"DEAR FRIEND"

Thos. Garrett   W Still

"DEAR FRIEND"

Thomas Garrett & William Still

Collaborators on the Underground Railroad

JUDITH BENTLEY

Illustrated with photographs & old prints

COBBLEHILL BOOKS/Dutton
New York

Illustration Credits

Courtesy of Chester County Historical Society, West Chester, Pa., 62 (photo by Jacob Hurn); Friends Historical Library of Swarthmore College, 108; Historical Society of Delaware, *ii* (left and lower left), 12, 17, 18; Historical Society of Pennsylvania, 43; The Library Company of Philadelphia, *ii* (right and lower right), 5, 8-9, 25, 26, 31, 39, 48, 49, 53, 61, 64, 70, 73, 74, 104; Reproduced from the Collections of the Library of Congress, 40, 75, 85, 92; Rutgers University Libraries, Special Collections & University Archives, 32-33.

Library of Congress Cataloging-in-Publication Data
Bentley, Judith.
    "Dear Friend" : Thomas Garrett & William Still, collaborators on the underground railroad / Judith Bentley ; illustrated with photographs & old prints.
        p.   cm.
    Includes bibliographical references (p. 111) and index.
    Summary: Based on correspondence between William Still and Thomas Garrett demonstrating the efforts of these two men to help slaves to freedom.
    ISBN 0-525-65156-X
    1. Underground railroad—Juvenile literature. 2. Abolitionists —United States—Biography—Juvenile literature. 3. Garrett, Thomas, 1789-1871—Juvenile literature. 4. Still, William, 1821-1902—Juvenile literature. [1. Underground railroad. 2. Abolitionists. 3. Garrett, Thomas, 1789-1871. 4. Still, William, 1821-1902. 5. Afro-Americans—Biography.] I. Title.
E450.B46   1997   973.7'115—dc20   96-27989   CIP   AC

Published in the United States by Cobblehill Books
an affiliate of Dutton Children's Books,
a division of Penguin Books USA Inc.,
375 Hudson Street, New York, New York 10014

Designed by Joy Taylor

Printed in the United States of America
First edition 10 9 8 7 6 5 4 3 2 1

Acknowledgments

I would like to acknowledge the help and inspiration of James McGowan, publisher of *The Harriet Tubman Journal* and author of *Station Master on the Underground Railroad, The Life and Letters of Thomas Garrett* (Moylan, Pa: The Whimsie Press, 1977). Jim is an expert on Garrett, Harriet Tubman, and the Eastern Line of the Underground Railroad.

Equally expert on William Still is Philip Lapsansky, Curator of the African-Americana Collection at the Library Company of Philadelphia. Phil provided photographs, documents, and particularly his own knowledge of 1850s Philadelphia.

Also contributing to this book were Ellen Rendle, the Historical Society of Delaware; Pamela C. Powell, Chester County Historical Society; Frances Cloud Taylor; and Jean de Mocko's reading class at Tillicum Middle School; Randall Nelson and Paula Laine, South Seattle Community College Library. Thanks to Rosanne Lauer for being a patient editor.

Contents

"DEAR FRIEND"

Esteemed Friends

TWO children had already been sold. The master intended to take four more to work on his plantation in Mississippi. What could a slave mother do?

"It almost broke my heart," Ann Marie Jackson recounted, "when he came and took my children away as soon as they were big enough to hand me a drink of water." She would never see the two who had already been sent from the southern Delaware farm to toil on richer soil in Mississippi. But she would not stand still and watch four more be carried away.

In the years before the Civil War, a slave mother had no good choices. The children's father was a free man, but children born to slave women became slaves, too. The father could only give them a last name and could do nothing to protect them. He felt so hopeless after the two children were taken that in the fall of 1858 he went crazy and died. In November his widow decided she would try to escape on her own, entrusting her fate and her children to the hands of strangers.

Two men in particular, one white and one black, were known to be helping fugitives. Mrs. Jackson had heard the name of Thomas Garrett, an iron and coal merchant in Wilmington, a town near the border with Pennsylvania. His name was whispered by slaves and muttered by slaveowners because he would always help runaways. With this meager plan, Mrs. Jackson gathered her seven remaining children, ages three to sixteen, and ran north toward Wilmington.

Such scraps of information — a name, a direction, a description of a gate — encouraged thousands of slaves like the Jacksons to flee the South in the 1850s. The scraps were clues to an escape route, a network of people known as the Underground Railroad. Some houses on the Underground did have tunnels and trapdoors, and sometimes the fugitives did ride on trains, but the "Underground Railroad" was mainly people who thought slavery was wrong. They were willing to help with a meal, a hiding place, or a ride.

Thomas Garrett was the Underground stationmaster in Wilmington, Delaware, on the Eastern line of the Underground. His station was the last stop on a route that drew fugitives from southern Delaware, Maryland, and Virginia. Garrett always seemed to know when passengers were coming. By 1858, he had already helped more than a thousand slaves escape. He would guide them the last few miles north to the border with Pennsylvania, then over the Mason-Dixon line, to freedom.

As the Jacksons made their way toward Garrett, they were helped by the many free blacks who lived in northern Delaware. In small towns and farms the Jacksons were hidden in houses, barns, or sheds during the day and transported at night to the next

Mother Escaping with Seven Children

safe spot. News of their movement traveled ahead of them, but when the family reached the outskirts of Wilmington, they were stopped. The Chesapeake and Delaware Canal south of the city stretched the width of the state, forming a barrier to a family trying to cross unnoticed. Word was passed to Thomas Garrett.

"They could not travel far on foot," Garrett wrote five days later to a friend in Philadelphia, "and could not safely cross any of the bridges on the canal, either on foot or in carriage." They must have taken a boat across, supplied by Garrett or Underground workers. Then he dispatched a man with a carriage to meet them.

"Owing to spies," Garrett continued to his "dear friend," the

5

family did not reach the man with the carriage "till 10 o'clock last night; this morning he returned, having seen them about one or two o'clock this morning in a second carriage on the border of Chester County, where I think they are all safe..."

Garrett's help with the journey was almost finished. The family would be safe in Chester County because it was over the line separating slave states from free. The merchant had many friends and relatives there who would provide shelter to his passengers. When night fell again, the Jacksons would go on to his brother's home in Upper Darby and then perhaps to Mrs. Jackson's brother in New Jersey, who was also an escaped slave.

"If you see them they can tell their own tales..." Garrett closed his letter. "May he who feeds the ravens, care for them."

Although he would never see them again, the stationmaster was hardly leaving the family's fate to God. His letter would alert a black man in Philadelphia to look out for them in case there was any more trouble. Just as Thomas Garrett's name was known in Delaware, William Still's name was known on the streets of Philadelphia.

The letter about the Jacksons was just one of many that passed furiously between these two men in the 1850s. The collaborators made an unlikely pair. Garrett was a sixty-five-year-old Quaker merchant with a genial smile but fearless demeanor. Still was a much younger man who was largely self-educated. They came from different families, one descended from English landowners, the other from Africans who had been forced into slavery. Yet both were driven by a desire to work in what Garrett called "the cause of the oppressed."

Still worked for an organization of both black and white abolitionists who wanted to abolish slavery. They were called the Philadelphia Vigilance Committee because they were "vigilant" in aiding fugitives. The white community provided money, and Still's job was to give it out. He would welcome the Jacksons, provide food, clothing, medical care, a place to stay, and transportation farther north if they needed it. He would also ask them questions: Who had their master been? What was their life in slavery like? Why had they escaped?

The Jacksons did pass through Philadelphia and Ann Marie impressed Still greatly. He wrote down that she had a pleasant countenance, humble bearing, and intellect above average. Resting in the committee's office on North Fifth Street, she confided that worry about her children's safety, as well as fear of their sale, had caused her to flee.

"Many times in going out to do days' work she would be compelled to leave her children, not knowing whether during her absence they would fall victims to fire, or be carried off by the master," Still recorded. "It was a special pleasure to aid such a mother."

Most newcomers from the South could melt into the neighborhoods and alleys of the bustling, interracial seaport of Philadelphia. They found work loading or unloading on the docks, pushing carts, or cleaning houses. Under the Fugitive Slave Law of 1850, however, slaveowners had the right to pursue escaped slaves into the free states and enlist the help of the police, judges, and ordinary people in recapturing them. For some runaways, it was dangerous to linger in the city.

A week after sending the Jacksons to Still, Garrett wrote again with urgent news: their master had come after them.

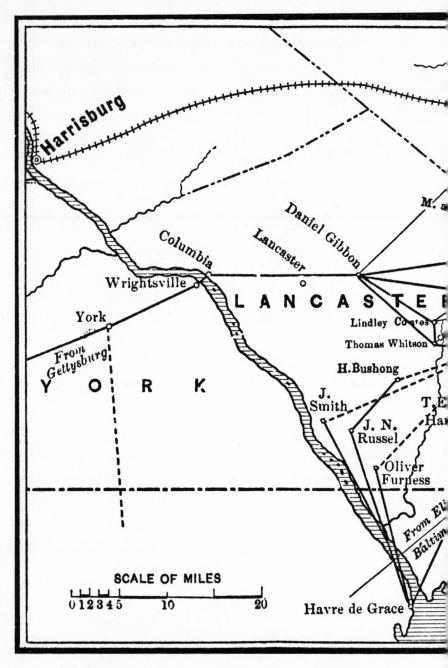

Map of Underground Railroad routes in Pennsylvania and Delaware, from William Siebert book.

MAP

showing the lines of the

UNDERGROUND RAILROAD

IN

Chester and the Neighboring
Counties of Pennsylvania

*Based on R. C. Smedley's History of
the Road in these Counties*

9

"Esteem'd Friend," Garrett wrote in haste, "A colour'd man has just come up from Dover on the Carrs [train], and says the woman's Master came up in the same Carrs..." On his way, the master had a black man arrested on suspicion of having helped the family. Perhaps from him, the master had heard that Ann Marie was going to her brother's in New Jersey. If he found her there, Garrett worried that the brother and others who had helped the family might be captured, too.

"I think it most likely you have seen her, and can tell where they are," he wrote to Still. "It's very important that they should be got out of the way, as, should she be taken, she may be the means of having several other colour'd persons convicted that assisted her. Do use the necessary means to get them out of the way...I have not time to write more at present, thy friend, T.G."

"Out of the way," in this case, meant all the way to Canada. The United States' northern neighbor was the only sure haven in the 1850s. Under British law, slavery was illegal there, and slave-owners or slavecatchers couldn't cross the border in pursuit.

By the time Garrett wrote the second letter, the Jacksons were well on their way on a train through New York State to the border. William Still received a letter dated November 30th from a minister in Canada saying the family had arrived, "safe and in good health and spirits." No doubt, he passed the good news back to Garrett in Wilmington.

The Jackson family settled into the free black community on the Canadian side of the border, and neither Garrett nor Still mentioned or saw them again. Among the fugitives they helped each day, Ann Marie Jackson's courage stood out, but many more were coming who needed their help. The freedom and lives of hundreds of passengers rested briefly on the bond these two men formed.

Few workers on the Underground Railroad kept written records of their actions. Because of the risk of fines and imprisonment, the work "called for still tongues." Garrett and Still, however, kept their pens busy. From his store in Wilmington, Garrett wrote several letters a day, often to Still. In the committee's small office, Still made detailed notes of each fugitive he interviewed. Garrett destroyed the letters he received from Still, but Still kept Garrett's.

Because Still had the instincts of an historian, those letters and notes survived the tumultuous years of the Civil War and the tense decades afterward. Today, the words they wrote reveal both the harrowing tales of fugitives like the Jacksons and the steadily developing trust between two men of different races united in a common cause.

Bass Otis portrait of Thomas Garrett, 1838

2

Thomas Garrett of Wilmington

ONE snowy December morning in 1845, a free black man and four fugitive slaves trudged into Thomas Garrett's iron and hardware store with a letter from a friend. The free man, Samuel Burris, was a guide who had led the fugitives twenty-five miles during the night from an Underground station farther south. Garrett greeted the chilled and exhausted men, added four more marks to his tally of fugitives helped, and quickly sent them on. But the letter meant trouble.

It came from John Hunn, a younger man who was part of the Quaker network in northern Delaware. He was writing about a family of fugitives who had not come on with the four. Yet they had all arrived at his house the day before.

"On the morning of the 17th of 12th month, 1845, as I was washing my hands at the yard pump," he later recounted, "I looked down the lane, and saw a covered wagon slowly approaching my house. The sun had just risen, and was shining brightly...on the snow which covered the ground to the depth of six inches...This seemed rather an early hour for visitors..."

The "visitors" were the Hawkins family from Queen Anne's County, Maryland: Sam Hawkins, a free man; his wife, Emeline, a slave; and their six children, ranging in age from eighteen months to sixteen years. For several years Sam Hawkins had tried to buy his wife's freedom, but her owner wouldn't sell, so they decided to flee. With the help of Burris, his wagon and horse, they had reached free blacks in Camden, Delaware.

There the four other men had joined the escape, and a Quaker gave them a letter of introduction in the next town. Traveling all night through a heavy snowstorm, the woman and children in the wagon and the men and boys walking twenty-seven miles, the thirteen had arrived in the morning.

"[T]he wanderers were gladly welcomed, and made as comfortable as possible until breakfast was ready for them," Hunn said. They had not planned to linger, but the deep snowfall made the roads difficult, so they all settled in the house and barn to rest for awhile.

Unfortunately the wagon had been seen. That afternoon the town constable dropped by with several strange men. In their hands was an advertisement that offered $1,000 for the recovery of some runaway slaves. Could they be in Hunn's house? the men asked.

At that moment, Samuel Hawkins came out of a building near the barn, and seeing the men, he ran. They gave chase, but Hawkins changed his mind about running and doubled back to the house with a knife, prepared to fight. Stepping into the fray, Hunn persuaded Hawkins to give up the knife and the constable to give up his pistol. Negotiations began.

The slavehunters wanted the two teenage sons who had been born to a slave mother, but their father, of course, didn't like that idea. Hawkins didn't want to turn over his younger children either; he argued that they should be free because they were born after he and his wife began living in a cabin of their own. Since the questions were complicated, Hunn suggested that all go to Middletown on his sleigh to see a judge.

There the slavehunters struck a deal. If Hawkins would give up the two older boys, the rest of the family would be allowed to continue. Although Hunn didn't trust the agreement, he had the mother and children brought to town. As he had feared, the whole family was sent to jail, eighteen miles away in New Castle.

Much distressed by the outcome, Hunn returned home where Burris and the four undiscovered fugitives were preparing to leave for Wilmington. Hunn sent along the letter: What should be done? From then on, the family's fate was in Thomas Garrett's experienced hands.

The call for help came as no surprise to the merchant; he had been helping fugitives for twenty years. The antislavery cause was his life's work, a cause he made part of his business, his religion, his family and friends.

Garrett's concern for justice had started early. His ancestors were Quakers who had emigrated from England in 1684, seeking religious liberty. The Garretts settled on land originally granted to William Penn in what became Pennsylvania.

As Thomas was growing up in the early 1800s, slavery was illegal in the state. He heard Friends (Quakers) rise in meetings and speak on the evils of slavery, which was still too close to their homes to ignore. Slaveowners from the nearby states of Delaware and Maryland often came into Pennsylvania after fugitives who had escaped, offering rewards to slavehunters who could help catch them. His own family had hidden runaway slaves at their farmhouse in Upper Darby.

Returning there one day about 1813, a young Garrett found his mother and the servants in an uproar. A free black woman working in the home had been snatched by a kidnapper with a wagon, and they were afraid she would be falsely claimed as a slave. Thomas immediately started in pursuit, following a distinctive track made by the wagon wheels. As he rushed after the wagon, Garrett had a vision.

A fundamental Quaker belief is that all human beings have some measure of "Inward Light," by which they experience God. Thus all human beings are equal in the eyes of God. As Thomas was following the kidnapper, "a light above the brightness of the sun shone in upon his soul," a friend related. The light revealed to Garrett the evil of slavery "as he had never before seen it. It was borne in upon his mind so vividly as to appall him, and he seemed to feel a voice within telling him that his work in life must be to help and defend this persecuted race."

Garrett caught up with the wagon, retrieved the woman, and returned to the household "rejoicing." From that moment on, he never said no to a fugitive needing help.

That same year Garrett married Mary Sharpless. In 1822, they moved to the new town of Wilmington with their first three children and built a home just a few blocks up from the waterfront at

A view of Market Street, Wilmington, Delaware, in 1850s.

227 Shipley Street. Garrett opened an iron, steel, and coal store, and his business grew as the town became a city.

Perhaps Garrett had moved for business reasons, but he also placed himself right in the path of fugitives fleeing to the North. Wilmington was perched at the top of a slave state like an inverted funnel, scooping up fugitive slaves from southern Delaware, Virginia, and the Eastern Shore of Maryland, and channeling them through a narrow corridor farther north. Garrett had already joined the new Pennsylvania Society for Promoting the Abolition of Slavery, and he continued to attend their meetings from just across the border.

Rachel Mendinhall Garrett

After only six years in the city, Mary died, a year after the birth of the couple's fifth child. Two years later Garrett married Rachel Mendinhall, whose father was also a Quaker merchant and abolitionist. Their only child, a son Eli, was born in 1831.

Rachel and Thomas's marriage lasted thirty-eight years, but little is known about her. She remained in the background of Garrett's Underground work, occasionally lending a bonnet or dress for a disguise. She may have been in poor health much of the time, but their home on Shipley became known as a haven. Together they sheltered fugitives, and Garrett made arrangements for their travel and paid expenses out of his own pocket. He even began counting the fugitives he helped and announcing his tally in Anti-Slavery Society meetings.

So there was never any doubt, when Hunn wrote to the older man, that Garrett would help the Hawkins family if he could. After sending off the four fugitives north, Garrett hurried south to New Castle.

Fortunately for Garrett, while the family was in jail, the slave-hunters had been sent out of town to get a legal document. Garrett interviewed the family, consulted with a lawyer and then persuaded a judge to free them. Knowing the slavehunters would not be happy when they returned, he asked the judge if he could hire a hack for the family.

"Here is a woman with a babe at her breast," Garrett told him, "and the child suffering from white swelling on its leg; is there any impropriety in my getting a carriage and helping them over to Wilmington?"

The judge said no, that would be all right.

Garrett told the driver he was only paying for the woman and the young children, that the two teenage sons born in slavery could walk. Exhausted by their ordeal, however, the whole family got in. The driver dropped them off in front of Garrett's store in Wilmington the same day. They went inside, and Garrett paid the driver $1.50.

At that moment, he committed the crime of "knowingly harboring" fugitives. He could have transported the mother and children but not the two teenage sons he "knew" to be slaves.

After another cold journey at night, the Hawkins family was well into safety in Pennsylvania, but their successful escape was costly to both Hunn and Garrett. A year later both men were sued by the slaveowner for helping the fugitives escape.

The lawsuit was not really surprising because Garrett had made no secret of his antislavery work. Nearby slaveowners often blamed him for the "property" they had lost. So far, he had not been harmed, but one enraged owner had told Garrett if he ever came South, he would shoot him.

"Well," said Thomas, calmly, "I think of going that way before long, and I will call upon thee."

And he did; he called on the man.

"How does thee do, friend?" said Garrett. "Here I am, thee can shoot me if thee likes." Face to face with the abolitionist, the slaveowner backed down.

Garrett thought it might be his "plain Quaker garb" or his "cool impudence" that kept him from harm. His friends thought it was his absolute fearlessness. "With his broad-brimmed hat, long and well-rounded Quaker waist-coat, telling of good digestion," wrote one, "he must have been a man to inspire respect for his prowess."

But in the trial of 1848, slaveowners wanted revenge. Both Hunn and Garrett were found guilty of the charges against them. Hunn was assessed $2,500 and Garrett $5,400 for costs of the trial and the value of the slaves.

Slaveowners in Maryland and Delaware celebrated the verdict, thinking they had shut Garrett down. "We hope that this severe punishment would remove the rails from the underground railway," wrote the Democratic newspaper in town. The trial seemed to have the opposite effect, however. The publicity made the location of Hunn's house well known to fugitives and Garrett's name even more famous.

Despite the fine, he vowed to continue. According to stories handed down over the years, a marshal warned Garrett, "Thomas, I hope you will never be caught at this business again."

"Friend, I haven't a dollar in the world," Garrett replied, "but if thee knows a fugitive who needs a breakfast, send him to me."

Garrett could no more abandon his abolitionist work than he could abandon his self-respect. "I should have done violence to my convictions of duty," Garrett said after the trial, "had I not made use of all the lawful means in my power to liberate those people, and assist them to become men and women, rather than leave them in the condition of chattels." He vowed to add a second story to his house to shelter more fugitives, if necessary.

By the early 1850s Garrett's list had reached 1,853. He was more than sixty years old, a time when his life might have slowed down. But in the years to come, his mission became more urgent. The Fugitive Slave Law was passed in 1850, as part of a compromise between the southern and northern states. The law said slaveowners could not only continue to pursue fugitives in the North but could also require sheriffs and other officials to help them.

Under the threat of more confrontation and a need for more secrecy, Garrett began a new correspondence with an activist in Philadelphia. In 1855, in response to a query about some fugitives, Garrett wrote his first known letter to the man he addressed as "Esteemed Friend, Wm. Still…"

3

William Still of Philadelphia

WILLIAM STILL had been working in the Anti-Slavery Society office in Philadelphia for three years in August, 1850. Although he started as a janitor and clerk, his employers soon realized he had greater abilities and valuable contacts in the black community. He started talking to fugitives when they came through the office and deciding who needed help. That summer day a white-haired black man was brought in.

The stranger was introduced as Peter Friedman, an ex-slave who had been wandering the city's streets searching for "his people." Friedman had journeyed 1,600 miles—all the way from Alabama—to find his family. He asked everyone he met about an old man and woman who had lived near the Delaware River, and a minister finally told him to ask William Still at the Anti-Slavery office.

Coming all the way from Alabama was unusual, but trying to find lost relatives was not. Still had heard such requests before, so he simply asked the stranger to tell his story. Friedman began talking in an earnest manner as William recounted later: "He and an older brother had been stolen away from somewhere in this direction, about 41 or 42 years ago, when he was a boy only about six years old. Since that time he had been utterly excluded from all knowledge of his parents, having never even so much as heard a word from them or any of his relatives." Before he was stolen, however, his grandmother had told him never to forget that his mother, father, and two sisters lived up north by the Delaware River.

Although his brother had died in slavery, Peter had never given up hope of seeing his parents again. He had come to Philadelphia to look for their names in church records or for people who remembered them. The trail seemed very cold, but Still wanted to help and continued asking the usual questions.

What were his parents' names?

"Levin and Sidney," Peter replied. He never knew their last name.

How had he escaped from slavery?

When his older brother died, Peter had vowed that he would not die a slave, too. With his owner's permission he had hired himself out to work for other people for pay. Then he arranged to be sold to a Jewish merchant named Joseph Friedman. Although Alabama law forbade slaves buying their own freedom, Friedman allowed Peter to gradually earn enough money to buy himself. Then the self-purchase was actually made in Cincinnati, Ohio, where it would be legal. Peter took Friedman's last name since he did not know his own.

He did remember a sister's first name, "Mahalah."

Still was startled. "That's not a common name," he replied. Did

Peter Still

Peter remember anything else?

"Yes," he did. His mother had a mole or a dark spot on her cheek. Suddenly, his family's history filled William's mind.

His own mother, Charity, had constantly prayed for two young sons she left behind in slavery when she fled the Eastern Shore of Maryland. Her husband, Levin, had decided before he turned twenty-one that he would die rather than remain a slave. He worked to buy his freedom, then moved to the free state of New Jersey and waited for his family to join him.

Charity Still

Charity managed to escape with her two young daughters and two sons, all younger than eight, but they almost starved on the way. Reaching New Jersey, they were reunited with Levin for a few months, but Charity's trail was followed. A gang of slave-hunters found the family and returned the slave mother and her children to Maryland.

A month later, Charity tried again, but this time she left the two sons behind with their grandmother. Hard as it was to leave them, she did not think she could make it once again with four children. The second escape worked, but her owner was angry and sold her two sons south. She had never seen them again.

As the couple settled in New Jersey, fourteen more children were born, including the youngest, William. His father had died in 1842, and Charity was a widow in her seventies, living on the small family farm.

William knew the family secrets—that his mother and two of her grown children had been fugitives themselves, that two more were "lost." "By this time I perceived that a most wonderful story was about to be disclosed," Still wrote later. The stranger standing before him, staring him "too full in the face...to dispute the evidence for one moment [was his] own dear brother whom I had never before seen....

"I could see in the face of my newfound brother the likeness of my mother."

His feelings at that moment were "unutterable," and he hid them for an hour until he could be sure of Peter's identity. After many more questions, "I took Peter and seated myself by his side," and told him calmly what had happened to his family. His mother had changed her name from Sidney to Charity to disguise her identity when she escaped. In New Jersey his parents had taken the last name of Still. Peter had six other brothers and sisters remaining.

Much to Still's surprise, Peter did not seem excited by the news. In fact, he was wary; he feared a trap. Slaveowners often warned slaves that the northern abolitionists could not be trusted. This lucky encounter seemed too good to be true.

That night William took the skeptical Peter to stay with their sister Mary, who operated a school for black children in

Philadelphia. Two days later, when they went to meet his mother in New Jersey, Peter finally believed he had found his family. He could see, too, that he looked like his mother.

"I shall not attempt to describe the feelings of my mother and the family on learning the fact that Peter was one of us," Still wrote to a white abolitionist, J. Miller McKim. "I will leave that for you to imagine."

Over the next few weeks, Peter caught up on the nearly fifty years of family history he had missed. The Stills' life had been free but hard. For one dollar they bought an acre of land surrounded by dense pine woods near the village of Indian Mills in Burlington County, New Jersey. The small farm provided some food, and Levin worked at the sawmill in the village, but work was seldom steady. Many times there was hardly any food in the house. William did chores and odd jobs to help out; he learned to chop and stack a full cord of wood in six hours.

The family was always secretive about their past. If Charity's identity were known, even the children born in freedom could be claimed by her old owner because they were the children of a slave mother. William knew the constant fear of being only miles away from slavery. Even close to their cabin, slavehunters had traced an escaped slave to the residence of an old man, Thomas Wilkins. When they broke into his home and began beating the runaway, Wilkins threw a shovelful of burning coals from his fireplace into their faces. When the slavehunters ran off, William Still had helped take the badly beaten fugitive twenty miles through the woods to a safe station on the Underground.

More than anything, as a child, William wanted to learn to read and write. He could not attend school regularly, sometimes because he had to work and sometimes because the teacher humiliated black children. Finally when he was seventeen, a new teacher took an interest in him and spent hours listening to him read. William began reading while he drove the family wagon and even as he chopped wood. At the age of twenty-three, he left home to join his older sisters Mary and Kitturah and look for work in Philadelphia.

In the decades before the Civil War, Philadelphia had the largest black population in the United States. Fugitives arrived from the South almost daily, and they were woven into the city's fabric through the efforts of fellow blacks. Most lived on the northern and southern fringes, the freestanding homes of prominent blacks mixing with the small attached houses of the poor and working class. Housing clustered around the docks, streets, and major roads, hotels and lodging places where jobs could be found.

Young Still arrived in the city with three dollars, so the story goes. Good jobs were scarce, but he believed that hard work would overcome poverty and prejudice. He worked first in a brickyard, then hauling wood. He opened an oyster-cellar serving hot broth, but that earned little. After brief stints selling secondhand clothes, digging wells, and working as a waiter, he was offered a job as a household servant for a wealthy widow, Mrs. E. Langdon Elwyn. She was an exacting employer, but she encouraged his love of books, and within three years, Still also taught himself to write.

In the fall of 1847, Still heard that a clerk was wanted at the Anti-Slavery Society office on North Fifth Street. The Society was the strongest of several abolitionist ventures in Pennsylvania, and its office had become the hub of antislavery activity. Visitors dropped in to buy books and read abolitionist pamphlets. The editorial offices of an abolitionist newspaper, *The Pennsylvania Freeman,* were located there, with a former Presbyterian minister, J. Miller McKim, as business manager and publisher.

The Society's first headquarters had been burned down by a mob in 1838, and abolitionists' words had been greeted with eggs, tomatoes, and bricks at first, but by the late 1840s their speeches and deeds had gradually aroused public opinion against slavery. William Still saw an opportunity in the Society's job. Although the salary offered was small ($3.75 a week), he would be paid for doing satisfying work. "I go for liberty and improvement," he said in taking the job, "esteeming it no small honor to be placed in a position where I shall be considered an intelligent being...." He was hired as a combination janitor and mailclerk, working for McKim.

When members of the Society discovered how capable Still was, his duties and salary increased. Then in his late twenties, Still was described by a journalist who met him as "somewhat tall, neat... [with] a smiling face...and gentlemanly." Even a slaveholder described him as "a devilish likely fellow...I saw him write a hand that I coul[d]n't beat....that William Still is a fine fellow."

The same year he began at the Anti-Slavery office, Still met and married Letitia George. She worked as a dressmaker, but they also took in boarders in their home. Some of those "boarders" were fugitives, and gradually the couple's home became part of a network of safe hiding places within the city.

As William worked for the Society and their home became a haven, the Stills provided a rare link between the black and white communities which were attacking slavery in different ways. The mainly white Society did the public work of abolition while the black community took on the more secretive task of "vigilance," watching out for escaped slaves who had arrived in the city and

Frontispiece drawing of William Still

then the slaveowners and hired gangs who came after them. Henrietta Bowers Duterte, the first black woman undertaker in Philadelphia, hid fugitives in caskets and funeral processions. James J.G. Bias, a physician and clergyman, offered medical checkups as well as beds in his house. Women's groups raised money by sponsoring annual fairs. Announcements of the vigilance committee were read from the pulpits of black churches. By 1850, when Peter "Friedman" began asking those ministers questions, he was naturally directed downtown to his brother.

Their joyful family reunion did not end Peter's story. Like

Philadelphia Oct. 12th 1852

A.S. Offin

My Dear Peter:

We would be glad to hear what you are doing towards effecting the deliverance of your family I understood that you had written to McKiernon, to know of him, if he would not take three thousand Dols, for your family — if so, have you received any answer yet? O, how glad I should be to hear of that the price on your family had been reduced. say two thousand Dols. But I have but little hope of being gratified with such news.

Have you ascertained yet what your friends in Burlington & N.J. will do in the way of pecuniary means, providing you can buy them your family? I should like to come up some time before long and have an interview with some of the friends on the subject —

Mr. McKim Rec'd a Letter last Saturday from Rev. S.J. May, of Syracuse in which was a note from Mrs. Reynolds, which I will enclose to you. probably

Letter of William Still to Peter Still

32

you can understand it. I cannot.

My love to Mary & tell her she must go up to Mothers soon & give Sophia a seting back. James informed me, in a letter last Saturday, that Sophia had been giving some great insults to Mother, and he proposed going up some time this week. Poor fellow, he was trembling. He thought if you would only lay claim to your share of the property it would have a good attendency. I answered his letter yesterday, & advised him to go up & read the law to them in plain language. so that they may know exactly just what to depend upon. But I want Mary to go up just for Sophia's sake. Tell her, I will pay her fare providing she will go. She need not loose any time. She can leave Burlington on Saturday Morning & then return on Monday Morning. by all means prevail on her to go

My wife & Daughter are both well, & though they know nothing of my being in the act of writing this letter yet I will take the liberty to send their love to you.

Answer this letter soon & oblige

Yours Truly

Wm S.

many slaves and freedmen before him, he had left behind a family in slavery—his wife, two sons, and a daughter—in Alabama. The members of the Society immediately tried to help.

At McKim's request, William wrote about the reunion with his brother, and the story was published in an abolitionist newspaper. A Quaker named Seth Concklin was touched by Peter's appeal for help. Concklin volunteered to travel to Alabama and guide the family to freedom. Leaders of the Anti-Slavery Society knew the journey would be dangerous, but they let Concklin go.

Peter gave Concklin a token to take to his wife, Lavinia, so she would trust him. She did, and traveling by water, Concklin brought the family north to Indiana, a free state. There they were betrayed, however, by some citizens seeking a reward. They were all arrested, and Concklin was charged with breaking the new Fugitive Slave Law, which required northerners to cooperate in the return of fugitive slaves. All were transported back to Alabama, the family to slavery and Concklin to face trial. On the way down, Concklin either jumped or was pushed overboard, in handcuffs, and drowned in the Ohio River.

Concklin's death and the failure of the mission jolted the Anti-Slavery Society. While Peter began a speaking tour to raise $5,000 to buy his family, the Society decided on more vigorous action all around. It gave William Still more responsibility for directly aiding fugitives. As members of the Society raised money, he gave it out to pay room, food, clothing, medicine, and transportation costs.

In the committee's journal, Still at first only kept track of the money:

Shorter, carriage	*.50*
Laundry-washing for fugitives	*.31*

1 coat	*2.00*
1 pair of pants	*1.62*
shaving apparatus, blacking, and haircutting	*.60*
1 cab	*.37*
6 days board	*3.00*

The day he made the "wonderful discovery" of his own brother, however, his mission changed. "All over this wide and extended country," he realized, "thousands of mothers and children, separated by slavery, were in a similar way living without the slightest knowledge of each other's whereabouts." Maybe he could do something about that.

On his own time, often working in the evenings, Still began asking the fugitives their names, where they had come from, and the names of their masters. He asked them about their escape experiences and how severely they had been treated. He wrote down their stories so that others might be able to find their families separated by slavery.

His decision to keep detailed records was dangerous; the notebooks were written proof that he and others were aiding fugitives, but that didn't stop him. "While I knew the danger of keeping strict records...it used to afford me great satisfaction," he explained, "to take them down fresh from the lips of fugitives on the way to freedom, and to preserve them as they had given them."

Like a true historian, he began keeping, too, the letters others wrote to him. When Thomas Garrett wrote, alerting him to more of "God's poor" on the way, that letter, too, went into Still's boxes.

4

The Conductors

THE Market Street Bridge crossing the Christiana River into Wilmington was always closely watched. Slave owners or sheriffs coming after a fleeing slave knew the fugitive had to cross that river on the way north, so the bridge was a good place to post lookouts or make an arrest.

Other eyes watched the bridge, too. Thomas Garrett's office and home were only a few blocks from the river. Black and Irish laborers worked on the waterfront, hauling and carting merchandise through the young city's streets and alleyways. They reported what they saw and heard to Garrett.

He kept in touch with agents to the south of the bridge, too. Word was easily passed when families like the Jacksons and Hawkinses were on the way north. If fugitives were in danger, Garrett would send someone to intercept them and ferry them across the river, avoiding the bridge.

For the eyes, ears, and feet of the Underground, Garrett depended on many workers. Some were employees in his own business and household who could go on a midnight errand after a day's work was done. As Garrett began a regular correspondence with Still in 1855, not only letters went back and forth. Many of the letters were hand-carried, and Garrett introduced the guides as men who could be trusted.

George Wilmer carried a letter to Still the day after Christmas. "He is a true man, and a forwarder of slaves," Garrett wrote about Wilmer. "[He] has passed some twenty-five within four months."

Three months after Wilmer, Garrett sent Harry Craige to guide a fleeing man, woman, and two children: "Thee may take Harry Craige by the hand as a brother, true to the cause; he is one of our most efficient aides on the Rail Road, and worthy of full confidence."

"This evening I send to thy care four of God's poor," Garrett wrote to Still in 1857. "Severn Johnson, a true man, will go with them tonight by rail to thy house."

Wilmer, Craige, and Johnson are mentioned only once or twice in Garrett's letters. There were many seldom-named blacks like the three who risked their lives and often their freedom in the antislavery cause.

In the small Delaware towns south of Wilmington, free blacks who worked by day were willing to transport fugitives at night if they could find a horse. As the agent who gave out money for the Anti-Slavery Society, Still received such a request in 1858:

"We have Bin trying to rais money to By a horse but there is so few here that we can trust...," the letter reported; "we have a Road that more than 100 past over in 1857...ther is much frait [freight] pases over this Road, But ther has Ben but 3 conductors for sum time."

They needed a horse to pass fugitives on quickly; "one of our best men was nigh Cut [caught] By keeping of them too long, by not having means to convay them...."

Besides guides, the most daring workers on the Underground were the conductors who traveled into slaveholding areas where they would collect an escaping group of slaves and conduct them to freedom. If caught, the conductors, too, could be reenslaved, no matter how long they had been free.

Samuel Burris, the man who guided the Hawkins family, became a frequent conductor. He "piloted them himself, or was instrumental in directing hundreds of fugitives to me for shelter," John Hunn related. Although Burris escaped notice when the Hawkins family was caught, a few years later, he was caught and thrown into jail in Dover, Delaware, for fourteen months. John Hunn and Thomas Garrett "were as faithful to him as brothers" during this period, Still asserted, but they could not prevent his conviction for helping fugitives. Burris was sentenced to be sold as a slave to labor for seven years.

The Underground Railroad quickly came to his rescue. Since Garrett and Hunn were well known to slaveholders because of their trial in the Hawkins case, a man named Isaac A. Flint was enlisted to go to the auction where Burris was to be sold. Pretending to be a slave dealer, Flint went through the motions of inspecting the feet, head, legs, arms, and body of the "property." Outbidding dealers from Baltimore, Flint purchased Burris, signed the bill of sale, and then whispered to the conductor that he had been bought with "abolition gold."

Samuel D. Burris

Harriet Tubman

Free once more and vastly relieved, Burris was also intimidated by the constant threat of becoming a slave again. Although he and his family lived in the free city of Philadelphia, they moved far away to the new free state of California in 1852. This man who helped "hundreds" to escape, perhaps more than any other conductor, never again returned to the South.

Nevertheless, a steady stream of guides, conductors, and fugitives continued to pass through the back countinghouse of Garrett's store and the Anti-Slavery office in Philadelphia. Most famous of all was one indomitable black woman, Harriet Tubman. Still described her as a woman without equal in courage, shrewdness, and exertions to rescue her people.

Tubman had escaped by herself from a farm in Dorchester County on the Eastern Shore of Maryland in the 1840s. Lonely in freedom, she made frequent trips back to Maryland and freed well over one hundred slaves, including her brothers, sisters, and her parents. She passed through Garrett's office at least eight times in the decade before the Civil War. He first wrote about her in an 1854 letter to the Anti-Slavery office:

> *Wilmington, 12th mo. 29th, 1854*
> *We made arrangements last night, and sent away Harriet Tubman, with six men and one woman to Allen Agnews, to be forwarded across the country to the city. Harriet, and one of the men had worn their shoes off their feet, and I gave them two dollars to help fit them out, and directed a carriage to be hired at my expense....*

Again in May, 1856, Garrett mentioned to Still that, "Those four I wrote thee about arrived safe up in the neighborhood of Longwood, and Harriet Tubman followed after in the stage yesterday."

Abolitionists supported Tubman not only with places to hide and transportation to the next station but with money to finance her trips. If he had not seen her, Garrett would send a note to Still, telling Harriet to drop by his store.

In October of 1856, she had been gone for some time, recovering from an especially cold and wet mission. On her way south again, Tubman came into Garrett's store and was directed to the back countinghouse where he was writing.

"Harriet, I am glad to see thee. Thee looks much better than when I last saw thee," Garrett exclaimed.

"Yes, I thank you. I am now well, and God has sent me to you for money."

"Harriet, how is this?" Garrett continued in a teasing tone. "I expected thee would want a new pair of shoes, as usual, when thee has been on a journey. These I can give thee, but thee know I have a great many calls for money from the coloured people, and thee cannot expect much money from me."

"You can give me what I need, now," she replied. "God never fools me."

Harriet believed that God was protecting her on her missions, and Garrett may have believed it, too. He related to friends in Scotland that Harriet was asking for the exact amount of money they had just sent him for the antislavery cause.

"Harriet, has thee been to Philadelphia lately?...Has anyone told thee I had money for thee?" Garrett asked. Harriet insisted that "nobody but God" had told her he had money for her. Amazed, Garrett handed over the amount she needed, and Harriet was once more on a journey to bring out slaves.

A few weeks later, as she headed back north with a new escape party, some slaveowners from Maryland arrived in Wilmington and

Page from William Still's Vigilance Committee journal, showing entry for Harriet Tubman

began putting up handbills advertising rewards for the recapture of three slaves. They also left posters at all the railway depots and towns leading north through Delaware. The posters offered $2,600 for the three fugitives and another $12,000 for a person called "Moses," who was said to be leading them.

The posters were torn down by black residents as fast as they were put up, but Garrett was worried that anyone who had seen them might be tempted by the rewards. Everyone would be watching the Market Street Bridge.

Soon word came from South Wilmington that a party of slaves was ready to cross the Christiana River. Sure enough, they included Josiah Bailey, for whom $1,500 was offered; his brother Bill, for whom $300 was offered; Peter Pennington, worth $800; Eliza Nokey and one more. The party was guided by Harriet, who was known as Moses because she led her people to freedom. Such a large, valuable group could not cross the Market Street Bridge unnoticed.

With Harriet's party hidden and waiting south of the bridge, Garrett quickly thought up a plan. He may have turned to Patrick Holland, an Irish worker who owned a livery stable very close to the north end of the bridge. For sure, the next morning, two wag- onloads of bricklayers left town, riding down Market Street, across the bridge, singing and shouting as if they were going on an out- ing.

Late that evening, after dark, the bricklayers returned in even higher spirits, again singing loudly and acting as if they had been drinking all day. Below their feet, under the straw, lay six adults, not daring to move as the wagon approached a checkpoint. Distracted by the revelers, the police did not even bother to check under the straw.

A day or so later, on November 18, William Still made an entry in his account book:

Josiah & Wm. Bailey cash	*3.25*
Harriet Tubman	*2.50*

He sent them on, and soon a letter came from Oliver Johnson in the Anti-Slavery office in New York, saying the group had made it all the way to Canada, singing joyously as they crossed the border.

In just a few weeks, however, Garrett was worried about Harriet. He knew she had planned to go south again over the

Christmas holidays to free her sister. The sister had children who did not live with her, and she would not leave without them. But at Christmas they could visit her, and the family would have a rare chance to escape together.

When Tubman did not come through as expected and did not stop in Philadelphia either, Garrett very much feared "she is sick, or something has happened to her..."

Months passed, and Garrett still had not seen her. Then there was a betrayal on the Delaware Underground. A free black man who falsely represented himself as a conductor had led eight fugitive slaves to the Dover jail, in return for a reward. When the slaves realized where they were, however, they had escaped, hurling hot coals from the fire at the sheriff as they fled.

The incident threatened to disrupt the normal operations of the Road. The man who betrayed the eight, Thomas Otwell, also knew Harriet Tubman and some of the places she regularly stopped. Would he betray her, too, Garrett wondered? He wrote to Still.

Wilmington, 3rd mo. 27th, 1857

Esteemed Friend, William Still:

I have been very anxious for some time past, to hear what has become of Harriet Tubman. The last I heard of her, she was in the State of New York, on her way to Canada with some friends, last fall. Has thee seen or heard anything of her lately? It would be a sorrowful fact, if such a hero as she, should be lost from the Underground Rail Road...If thee gets this in time, and knows anything respecting her, please drop me a line by mail to-morrow, and I will get it next morning if not sooner, and oblige thy friend...

Thomas Garrett

Still wrote back to Garrett that Tubman was "all right," although she had not succeeded in bringing out her sister. Garrett was truly glad to learn that she was still in good health and "ready for action," but he asked Still to warn her that there would be more danger on the Road because of the escape.

Despite the warning, Harriet did go back again to bring out more fugitives, passing through Garrett and Still's offices several more times before the Civil War began. Still admired her adventurous spirit and attributed her success to an "utter disregard of consequences." No one like her, he said, had been seen "before or since." She never lost a passenger and was never caught. Despite all the stationmasters could do, however, not all the passenger runs were as successful.

5

Escape by Sea

WHILE most fugitives walked to freedom, hiding in the woods, crossing rivers, and stomping miles in the cold snow, others relied less on their feet. Early in his years working for the Anti-Slavery Society, William Still was on hand one morning when a wooden box bound with five hickory hoops was delivered by an express shipping company. Two feet eight inches deep, two feet wide, and three feet long, the box was from Richmond, Virginia, marked "This side up with care."

When the office door was locked, one of the members of the Society rapped quietly on the box's lid and called out, "All right?"

An answer came from within, "All right, Sir!"

The hickory hoops were cut, the lid lifted, and a young man looking very wet stepped out. Henry Brown, thereafter known as Henry "Box" Brown, reached out his hand with a "How do you do, gentlemen?"

Brown had been in the box for twenty-six hours. A white man

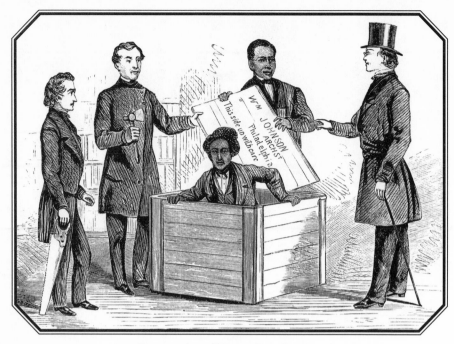

Resurrection of Henry Box Brown

named Samuel A. Smith, a shoe dealer in Richmond, had nailed up the box and sent his friend on his way. During one part of the trip, the box had been lodged upside down, putting Brown on his head. But he had survived with a few small biscuits, an animal bladder containing water, and a gimlet for making air holes.

Brown spent a few days recovering in abolitionists' homes, including Still's, and then moved on to Boston. His story, which caused a sensation in abolitionist newspapers, encouraged others to try a box or chest escape. An eighteen-year-old girl, Lear Green, escaping a forced marriage, stowed away in a chest as freight on the Ericsson line of steamers from Baltimore to Philadelphia. Another young woman who was pregnant traveled the same route in a box and barely survived the ordeal. Both women also recuperated in the Stills' home.

Lear Green Escaping in a Chest

Samuel Smith, too, heard of the success and helped box two more men for express shipment. When their absence was discovered, however, a telegram intercepted their boxes. Smith spent eight years in the Richmond penitentiary for the assistance he had given. When he was released in 1856, William Still helped draft a resolution by "the colored citizens of Philadelphia" thanking Smith for the good he had done.

Traveling in boxes was one of the more ingenious methods of escaping the South. Another was smuggling oneself onto a ship, with or without the connivance of the captain. Despite increasing tensions over the slavery issue, trade between the North and South continued during the 1850s. Thomas Garrett wrote frequently to Still about fugitives who had arrived in Wilmington on commercial vessels.

Wilmington, 3rd mo. 23rd, 1856

Dear Friend, William Still:

Captain Fountain has arrived all safe, with the human cargo thee was inquiring for, a few days since. I had men waiting till 12 o'clock till the captain arrived at his berth, ready to receive them.

The same captain came again in November of that year with an especially valuable load.

Wilmington, 11th mo. 4th, 1856

Esteemed Friends, J. Miller McKim and William Still:

Captain F. has arrived here this day with four able-bodied men. One is an engineer, and has been engaged in sawing lumber, a second, a good house carpenter, a third a blacksmith, and the fourth a farm hand. They are now five hundred miles from their home in Carolina, and would be glad to get situations, without going far from here....

Like the four Garrett mentioned, many of the fugitives who came by boat had worked in the seaports and learned a trade. Often they had hired themselves out, paying their masters a set amount but keeping some money for themselves. Thus they had gained a measure of independence and were able to pay for their passage.

Several captains were known to be willing to add fugitive slaves to their cargoes for a fee. One such was Captain "B," who owned a schooner. He would "bring any kind of freight that would pay the most," Still said, but he required at least three passengers, each paying a hundred dollars, before he would make the trip from Richmond to Philadelphia. He felt the risk of breaking the smuggling laws justified the fare.

Captain B's boat had "a very private hole" below the regular bottom of the deck where he hid fugitives, but he also had to remain above suspicion with his customers in Richmond. Once he brought away three slaves, one of whom had stolen $1,500 from his master the day he left. On a later trip to Richmond, Captain B happened to call at the oysterhouse kept by the slave's owner. The owner had received a boasting letter from the escapee in Canada, and he was furious. He offered Captain B $2,000 or more if he would find the fugitive and bring him back. The captain "was good at concealing his feelings," Still noted, and managed to deflect the offer without arousing suspicion.

The Captain Fountain mentioned in Garrett's letters was one of the most reliable captains in "human cargo" smuggling. In the four-year period from 1855 to 1859, Garrett mentions six trips Fountain made bringing at least fifty passengers. "Rough and rugged" in appearance, with a large head, large mouth, large eyes, and heavy eyebrows, Fountain was a man who never let what he was thinking or feeling appear on his face. Such muscle control proved useful one day in November, 1855.

His schooner was lying at the wharf in Norfolk, Virginia, loading wheat. Hidden in the hold were twenty-one fugitive slaves, sixteen men and five women, among them several "good mechanics," an "excellent dressmaker," and some "prime" waiters and chambermaids. Because they were valuable workers, their absence had already been noticed, and rumors were flying around the seaport. The mayor of Norfolk himself, with officers carrying axes and long spears, came onboard and demanded to inspect the ship. Captain Fountain agreed, and the men began spearing the wheat and axing the decks in a rather clumsy but destructive fashion.

At first the captain remained impassive as the boarding party chopped at his ship, but he soon saw a chance to intervene. Seizing the axes himself, he offered to open up whatever spot the mayor wanted. This one maybe? Or that spot over there? Fountain attacked the deck with such power that splinters flew from the boards. The mayor quickly decided enough was enough and called off the search. After paying the five-dollar search fee required of every vessel leaving Virginia, Captain F set sail for the North.

Evidently Still was expecting some of the twenty-one stowaways to reach Philadelphia, but there was some delay. When they did not arrive promptly, he wrote to Garrett, and Garrett explained that he had done all he could.

Wilmington, 11th mo. 21st, 1855

Esteemed Friend, Wm. Still:

Thine of this date, inquiring for the twenty-one, and how they have been disposed of, has just been received. I can only answer by saying, when I parted with them yesterday afternoon, I gave the wife of the person in whose house they were, money to pay her expenses to thy place. I gave her husband money to pay a pilot to start yesterday with the ten men, divided in two gangs; also I had to leave soon after noon yesterday to attend a brother ill with an attack of apoplexy, and to-day I have been very much engaged....I should think they have stopped to-day, in consequence of the rain, and most likely will arrive safe to-morrow....

Indeed they did. The next day Still noted that he had paid out $27.68, including board for six men, two carriages to Kensington (probably for lodging), the washing of eleven pieces of clothing, cash to six people, and money for one coat and two pairs of shoes.

The story of the twenty-one was not quite finished, however.

The Mayor and Police of Norfolk Searching Capt. Fountain's Schooner

At a meeting of the Pennsylvania Anti-Slavery Society a couple of weeks later, a discussion began about exactly how much money was being spent on fugitives and how many were being helped. A friend from Ohio at the meeting claimed that the whole state of Ohio was one big Underground Railroad, passing on as many as twenty people on one day. They hadn't heard much about the Eastern line, he said, whereupon a Pennsylvania member rose and pointed to Thomas Garrett, saying he had helped twenty-one just a few days before.

"Now I had no objection for all mankind to know that I would assist all in my power to freedom," Garrett wrote to a friend in Scotland, but he would not have mentioned a specific number.

"I fear it may prove to have been impertinent to name the number of twenty-one that had passed within three weeks, for this reason, three had come from Carolina & 18 from Norfolk in the same vessel, & the Norfolk people had a suspicion they had come this way, but had suspected two vessels that had left for New England on the day they were missed." They knew the eighteen were onboard one of the ships, and if they heard that number, suspicion might turn in Fountain's direction. Garrett's worry was apparently in vain; no one seems to have made the connections, and Captain Fountain continued his trade.

Although many of the sea fugitives were skilled workers who left their jobs and walked straight onto the boat, others escaped and hid in the swamps of Carolina and Virginia until a willing captain was in port. Garrett warned about one such passenger in 1857 who might need a delousing.

Wilmington, 11th mo. 25th, 1857

Respected Friend, William Still:

I write to inform thee, that Captain Fountain has arrived this evening from the South with men, one of which is nearly naked, and very lousy. He has been in the swamps of Carolina for eighteen months past....I would send them on to-night, but will have to provide two of them with some clothes before they can be sent by railroad....As most likely all are more or less lousy, having been compelled to sleep together, I thought best to write thee so that thee may get a suitable place to take them to, and meet them at Broad and Prime [Pine?] streets on the arrival of the cars, about 11 o'clock tomorrow evening....

Fugitives smuggled to Wilmington were often put ashore at Old Swedes Church where Garrett would send one of his guides like Severn Johnson to meet them. In Philadelphia, captains often chose to unload their secret passengers in the middle of the night. Still describes the scene near League Island, at the foot of Broad Street, on the night of July 4, 1856.

He had arranged for three carriages with trustworthy drivers to wait on the banks of the Schuylkill River where "all was quiet as a 'country graveyard.' The moon was shining and soon the mast of a schooner was discovered." As the schooner approached the bank, those on shore were tempted to shout but spoke only in whispers to determine the name of the captain and the ship. They decided to pull the passengers up the embankment from the deck of the ship "by taking hold of their hands as they stood on tip toe."

"One after another was pulled up, and warmly greeted," Still recalled, "until it came the turn of a large object, weighing about two hundred and sixty pounds, full enough to make two ordinary women." The first attempt to lift her failed, but with the captain pushing from behind, she was safely landed. The captain was happy to push; the ship had been searched twice on its way from Norfolk, and the large woman had been hard to hide.

When a ship captain assumed the risk of smuggling, he took certain precautions. It was usually safer to list Wilmington, a seaport in a slave state, rather than Philadelphia as a destination, for example. In dealing with officials, the ability to keep a straight face as Captain B did, or to act insulted as Captain Fountain did were useful skills. The weather, however, was uncontrollable, and laws in states like Virginia were very strict. If a captain was caught smuggling, punishment was certain.

In one of the largest escape attempts, seventy-seven slaves left Washington, D.C., for Philadelphia in a small craft called *The Pearl*.

The boat was apprehended, however, and its captain spent four and a half years in jail before being pardoned by President Millard Fillmore.

Another captain who operated out of Wilmington, Captain Lambdin, was described by Garrett as a "very intelligent young captain." He had successfully brought slaves at different times from the South, but in 1855, he left Norfolk in a hurricane with five fugitives onboard. In the high wind and seas, the vessel became disabled. To save everyone's life, the captain had to head back to Norfolk. A few miles from the seaport, the ship wrecked in full view of the beach. Lambdin had to give himself up, along with the fugitives. Although he argued that the slaves were on the ship without his permission, he was imprisoned and charged with attempting to carry slaves to the North. He faced a sentence of ten years in prison for each of the five slaves.

"The Captain has a young wife here, with one child, 15 months old, a sweet little creature," Garrett wrote to a friend. "I went to the wife, yesterday. I encouraged her to go on, so as to be there at the trial, & to take her babe along. I have pledged to raise 50 dollars towards furnishing lawyers to plead his cause…"

Captain Lambdin's wife left Wilmington in December, 1855. A few months later Lambdin asked for some books with arguments against slavery which he wished to use in his own defense. Garrett wrote to Still, asking for several books from the Anti-Slavery office, but he added that "His friends here think there is no chance for him but to go to the penitentiary."

Other than paying lawyers' fees and providing books, the two stationmasters were powerless to defend Lambdin. Still recounts that, "He had his trial, and was sent to the penitentiary, of course."

The fate of the five slaves was not mentioned and probably not known. Not until the Civil War would those who had been imprisoned and those who returned to slavery have a chance for release.

6

A Nest of Abolitionists

WHEN ship captains, conductors, and guides brought passengers to Thomas Garrett's doorstep, the fugitives were almost home free. For the last twenty-seven miles to Philadelphia, Garrett and Still had spun a thick web of Underground lines and stations that would carry them safely from slave state to free city.

The fastest way to Philadelphia was the train, which Garrett called "the cars," but the cars had some drawbacks. Only fugitives who would not be recognized could travel this route. Any railroad worker who knowingly transported fugitives could be fined by the state of Delaware. To avoid this problem, Garrett usually sent his passengers just over the state line to board the train at stations in Chester or Marcus Hook.

On February 5, 1858, for example, Garrett wrote to William Still about a group of "6 able-bodied men" who would "take the cars at Chester, and most likely reach the city between 11 and 12 at night....Hoping all will be right," he suggested that Still have someone at the station in Philadelphia to look out for them. Always reliable on his end, Still noted that the six arrived "as usual in due time."

Although the overland route was slower, it had some advantages. Some fugitives needed time in the countryside to rest their feet, to warm themselves, and eat. Others needed to get out of Wilmington secretly, in a hurry. "I had just commenced this letter," Garrett wrote to a friend in Scotland, "when two colored men called to say they had three fugitives at their house, all able-bodied men, not more than 15 miles from their master's...." The men needed to put more miles between them and the master immediately, so Garrett found a pilot to guide them to the house of "a friend in Chester Co."

There were many such friends in Chester County, just across the Delaware/Pennsylvania line. Indeed, Garrett said "the whole neighborhood there" were abolitionists. Many were his relatives: his cousins Benjamin Price and Samuel Rhoads, his brother Isaac and half-brother Samuel, and his wife's family, the Mendinhalls (spelled with an "i"). The first gatepost across the line belonged to one branch of his in-laws, Isaac and Dinah Mendenhall (who preferred an "e").

If a pilot was not at hand to take fugitives to the friend, Garrett might send a single man through Wilmington carrying a scythe or hoe or rake on his shoulder. He would tell the man to hide the tool under a certain bridge, leading out of town. Later the tool would be retrieved to be used by the next "laborer" passing through.

Once across the bridge, the traveler could follow the Kennett Turnpike northwest about ten miles. "Go on and on until you reach a stone gate post," Garrett would tell him, "and then turn in" to the Mendenhalls.

If the fugitive was a woman, Garrett might borrow his wife Rachel's scoop bonnet. Its large curving rim could easily conceal a face. One time a constable was hanging around the front of Garrett's home, hoping to spot a fugitive. Garrett stepped out with a woman dressed in a Quaker gown and bonnet and told the constable he was taking his wife to meeting. Instead, Garrett escorted the slavewoman all the way to the home of Samuel Pennock, another safe house across the line in Chester County.

Garrett needed every trick and friend he could rely on one October morning in 1855, when a party of eleven fugitives arrived in broad daylight. Harriet Shephard and her five children were fleeing from slavery in Chestertown, Maryland. The mother had enlisted five others to escape with them, an aunt and uncle and three young men. Since the children couldn't walk far, Harriet had borrowed the horses and carriages belonging to her master. They drove to the center of town, "looking as innocent as if they were going to meeting."

Such an unusual party naturally attracted attention, and they were soon reported to Garrett. He decided at once that the horses and carriages must be abandoned and the eleven whisked out of Wilmington. Telling the story later, William Still revealed his admiration for his friend. "With the courage and skill so characteristic of Garrett, the fugitives, under escort, were soon on their way to Kennett Square."

The Shephard party could be sure of a warm welcome in Kennett Square. The town was a haven for fugitives, part of the nest of abolitionists in Chester County. Members of the Kennett

Escape of Eleven Passengers from Maryland in Two Carriages

Monthly Meeting of Friends, like the Mendenhalls, Maria and Allen Agnew, and Dr. Bartholomew and Lydia Fussell, had long been active in opposing slavery. One resident had opened a free produce store, refusing to sell products made with slave labor.

For many years before the Underground was in operation slavery had been discussed in the Friends' meetings of Pennsylvania. By the early 1800s most meetings had decided that their members could no longer hold slaves themselves, but they were divided as to whether members should actively oppose slaveholding by others. Those who wanted to protest publicly and take a strong stand

Longwood Progressive Meeting of Friends photograph showing crowd of people in front, including William Lloyd Garrison, about 1855-65.

were admonished by more conservative Quakers. When the Kennett Meeting excluded a few members for their antislavery activities, they decided to form a new meeting, called the Longwood Progressive Meeting of Friends. John and Hannah Cox provided land for the new meetinghouse, which was completed in 1855.

The modest frame building soon became a place for speech-making. Well-known lecturers like the abolitionist William Lloyd Garrison, women's rights advocate Susan B. Anthony, and the poet John Greenleaf Whittier spoke on the issues of the day. One conservative newspaper described it as a place where "long-haired men and short-haired women" plotted revolution.

Garrett's hair was fairly short, but he and Rachel were founders and prominent members of the Longwood Meeting. "My wife and self were at Longwood today," Garrett wrote to Still on September 6, 1857, "had a pleasant ride and good meeting." The meetings for worship and lectures also provided connections to members who would hide and transport fugitives from one home to another.

Into this radical community came the eleven fugitives from Maryland—men, women, and children for whom slavery was more than an issue to discuss. They reached Longwood meeting-house in the evening while a meeting was in session. After staying awhile at the meeting, they remained all night with one of the Kennett friends.

By daylight they were brought to Kimberton, the home of Grace Anna Lewis. Lewis was the third of four daughters in a Quaker family that had always aided those most in need. Her father had died of typhus after treating two black people nobody else would help.

At the age of four or five, Grace Anna had seen a man bound with ropes and carried off to slavery, and she never forgot the agony on his face. At another time in her childhood, a white handkerchief was to be waved out a back window to warn a black fugitive working in the nearby woods if he was in danger.

When their mother died, too, the daughters carried on the tradition of hospitality and loyalty to the fugitive. With the help of the neighboring Fussells, to whom they were related, the Lewises passed passengers on to numerous stations. If the fugitives needed

Grace Anna Lewis

time to recover their health or earn money, many stayed to work for the sisters. If they needed a disguise or just new clothes, a sewing circle of trusted friends rapidly convened.

Forty fugitives had once passed through the Lewis home in one week without even arousing suspicion. A week later, the sisters were amused to hear the comment of one of their proslavery neighbors. He said that there used to be a pretty brisk trade of running off fugitives in the neighborhood, "but there was not much of it done now." Quite the contrary, the party of eleven was moving through his neighborhood, and coordination was needed.

William Still was not a Quaker. He was a member of the Central Presbyterian Church of Color in Philadelphia, but he kept in constant touch with what he called the "hotbed of abolition." He was the central brain in this Wilmington-Chester County-Philadelphia triangle, the person to contact when fugitives were on the road. Still also gave out the Society's money for train fare, so when the eleven arrived at her home, Grace Anna wrote to him immediately:

Kimberton, October 28th, 1855

Esteemed Friend:

This evening a company of eleven friends reached here, having left their homes on the night of the 26th....The case seems to us one of unusual danger, she said, because the group had left behind a woman who knew of their intention to flee and pass through Wilmington.

We have separated the company for the present...until I could write to you and get advice if you have any to give, as to the best method of forwarding them, and assistance pecuniarily, in getting them to Canada....We shall await hearing from you.

Still thought carefully about his choices. Not all fugitives on the eastern line of the Underground went straight from Wilmington to Philadelphia. Many bypassed the city, found work, and stayed on Pennsylvania farms. But a party that had stolen its master's horses and carriage was likely to be followed and could not linger.

Letters flew back and forth. The mother and children were sent off "of the usual route" to a place they could stay a few days. The aunt and uncle and three young men were sent to Elijah Pennypacker in Phoenixville. Pennypacker's home was the easternmost station in Chester County, the point where three Underground routes converged, one from the West and two from the South, including Wilmington.

If necessary, Pennypacker would be able to move the group quickly. He kept a large two-horse dearborn, a carriage with curtained windows, that would easily hide passengers. If he had a full load, he carried children covered up in the rear of a wagon, women disguised by wearing veils, and men walking singly so as not to excite suspicion. From his home fugitives could go east to Philadelphia, Norristown, or Quakertown or west to Reading or Harrisburg, and then north through New York State to Canada.

Pennypacker sent the three men on east to Norristown. According to Still's notes, the whole group of eleven was eventually forwarded to the committee in Philadelphia, then divided and disguised, and sent north by train.

With those notes, the paper trail ends for the Shephard family. Like many Still sent on, they probably passed through the hands of John W. Jones in Elmira, New York. An escaped slave himself, Jones had made an arrangement with some of the employees of the Northern Central Railroad which ran through Elmira. Escaping parties would enter the baggage cars at 4 A.M. for a journey to Canada across Niagara Falls. There, among the boxes and crates, five children would have felt uncomfortable but lucky as they bumped along to the border. Many ex-slaves in Canada wrote back to say they had arrived safely, but neither Still nor Garrett mentions the Shephards again. They could not linger over any one family.

The completion of steam railroads on the East Coast meant that many fugitives could be passed more quickly than ever over longer distances. It also inspired Still's correspondents to use bad puns as code language: "I suppose you are somewhat uneasy because the goods did not come safe to hand on Monday evening, as you expected—consigned from Harrisburg to you." wrote G.S. Nelson to Still in May, 1857. "The train only was from Harrisburg to Reading, and as it happened, the goods had to stay all night with us, and as some excitement exists here about goods of the kind, we thought it expedient and wise to detain them until we could hear from you. There are two small boxes and two large ones; we have them all secure; what had better be done? Let us know...."

Although the Underground continued to operate cautiously, fugitives were attracting more sympathy from residents of the free states. Garrett considered it safe, in many instances, to forward them in open day. With the fast tracks of the aboveground train added to the web of Chester County homes, the passengers and letters increased between Garrett and Still.

"My list now counts 2011 Slaves that I have been enabled to assist on their Northern journey," Garrett wrote in 1856. Two months later he recounted to a Longwood friend, "My slave list is now 2038. Still they go."

7

The Philadelphia Connection

THE month of November, 1857, strained all the resources of the eastern line of the Underground Railroad. Sixty fugitives were recorded in William Still's journal that month. Among them was a group of twenty-eight that passed through many of the usual hands: Thomas Garrett's in Wilmington, Grace Anna Lewis's in Chester County, Elijah Pennypacker's in Phoenixville, and finally through Still's in Philadelphia. As they came, their progress was reported from one station to the other:

"I write to inform thee that we have either 17 or 27, I am not certain which, of that large gang of God's poor, and I hope they are safe," Garrett wrote to Still.

"Eight more of the large company reached our place last night," Lewis wrote to Still.

Then Pennypacker told Still they had reached his station, and Still wrote back: "With regard to those unprovided for, I think it will be safe to send them on any time toward the latter part of this week."

Word of the November arrivals buzzed through the antislavery community. "Last week at the meeting the Pres. of the U.G. Railroad Thomas Garrett said he had been detained from the first sitting in order to pass on 21 who came in one company," one member wrote to another. "A friend with whom we were in Chester County the next day said they had been roused at midnight the night before to aid eleven whom an agent was bringing in three (?) wagons!"

Such large numbers moved safely by 1857 because the lines of communication between white and black abolitionists, between the Quakers in Chester County and the black community in Philadelphia, were firmly established. In the years before Garrett and Still started their correspondence, this had not been true.

Even though black and white abolitionists had advocated the same cause for years, they had not worked closely together. In large public gatherings such as the funerals of prominent leaders, the races might mingle. But when Lucy Stone lectured on women's rights to a large audience at Musical Fund Hall in Philadelphia, blacks could not be seated. In the churches, too, the seats were separate. Most of Philadelphia's leading black congregations were formed when some Protestant churches began sending blacks to the balconies or separate pews.

When the Anti-Slavery Society was founded, Robert Purvis, a wealthy and prominent man of mixed race, was a member. He served as its president for several years, but by the 1840s the Society had become largely white. In a manner typical of organizations, it then appointed a committee "to inquire into the cause of the diminution of interest among the colored people in respect to association with us." The cause was that blacks felt the societies

The Christiana Tragedy

spent too much time meeting and talking and writing and too little time helping real people.

That difference was obvious in a violent encounter called the Christiana Riot, which occurred in 1851, a year after passage of the Fugitive Slave Law in 1850. The law had alarmed blacks much more than whites because free blacks were afraid of being "recaptured," no matter how long they had been free. Even William Still's family knew this fear because his mother was an escaped slave. Blacks held massive protests, and Robert Purvis threatened to shed the blood of "any pale-faced spectre" who entered his dwelling "to executive [execute] this law on me or mine...."

Into this angry atmosphere strode Edward Gorsuch, a

Maryland slaveholder who came to Philadelphia in September, 1851, seeking four slaves who had escaped from his farm. Using his legal rights, he obtained warrants for their arrest. As was also his right, he hired two policemen and asked a federal marshal to help him find the four.

His actions did not go unnoticed. He was seen talking with a professional kidnapper named Kline and to a lawyer who was known to dabble "in negro-catching." A black man named Samuel Williams overheard them talking about the plans. First Williams told the Anti-Slavery office what he had heard, and then he began tailing Kline to find out exactly where he was going.

When he heard of Gorsuch's actions, William Still sent a warning to the four escaped slaves who were hiding in Christiana in Lancaster County. There had already been several kidnappings in that county, and black residents decided they would not stand by quietly this time. They armed themselves with guns, clubs, and corn-knives (long, heavy knives used for chopping down cornstalks).

Gorsuch and his posse arrived in Christiana at daybreak and broke into the house where two of the fugitives were hiding. As they climbed the stairs, the home's defenders blew a horn from an upstairs window; more than fifty blacks came running to help. Before he realized how outnumbered he was, Gorsuch was killed by the mob and his son badly injured. The two slaves escaped.

Thirty-eight people were arrested in the riot and charged with conspiracy to commit treason. When the first two people tried were found not guilty, the rest were released, too.

Despite this legal success, the violence of the encounter shocked the Anti-Slavery Society. In response, the Society decided to work more closely with black abolitionists. A General Vigilance Committee was formed; seven of its nineteen members were black. A four-man action group was given the task of dealing directly with fugitives. Naturally, the man who was even then a valuable link between the black and white communities became the action committee's chair.

Thereafter, whenever a stranger appeared in the city, word passed quickly through alleys and courtyards, from teamster to coachman, from waiter to dockworker, eventually to William Still. The larger committee provided the money to board fugitives with families of free Negroes, and Still knew where to find those families. One night alone, an Underground worker counted 168 fugitives being harbored in homes in the city.

The black-white partnership worked especially well in July of 1855. A southern slaveholder who had been named ambassador to Nicaragua, Colonel John H. Wheeler, passed through Philadelphia on his way to New York and then to his new position. He wanted to take Jane Johnson, a slavewoman, and her two young sons with him to Nicaragua. Wheeler's friends had warned him that bringing slaves through the city was risky. Under Pennsylvania law they would be free as soon as they entered the state. If Johnson knew that, she could leave her master.

Ignoring the warnings, Colonel Wheeler escorted Johnson and her sons from the South Broad Street train station, where they arrived, to Bloodgood's Hotel, where they would wait for the afternoon ferry to Camden, New Jersey. Wheeler went into the dining room to eat, and Jane Johnson was left sitting alone. Knowing her rights, Johnson whispered to a black woman in the hotel that she wished to be free.

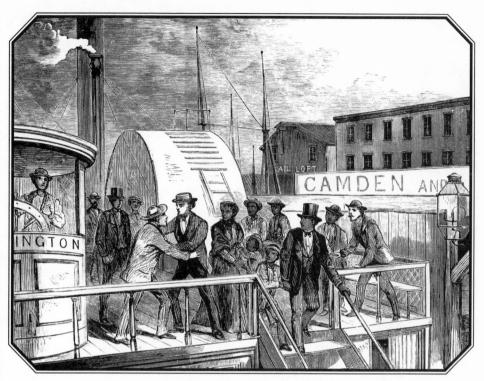

Rescue of Jane Johnson and her children

The word was quickly passed to Still at the North Fifth Street office. Before leaving the office, Still took the precaution of alerting Passmore Williamson, a young white lawyer on the action committee. After telling Williamson to meet him at the ferry, Still stopped on his way to the dock to hire a coach and recruit some help.

As the two abolitionists approached Johnson and her sons, a crowd of about a dozen black men quickly assembled near Wheeler. While Still spoke to Johnson, Williamson explained the situation to her owner as the men surrounded him. Someone put a hand on the Colonel while Johnson and her sons were guided to

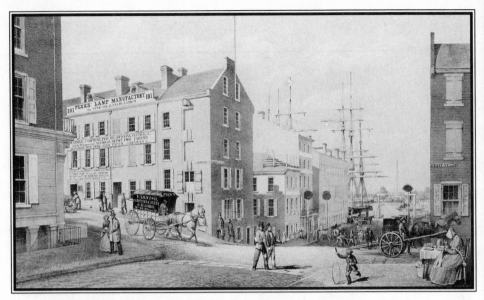

Bloodgood's Hotel at the end of Walnut Street, next to the water and ferry dock.

the waiting coach and taken to Still's home. The next day the three went on to New York and later to Boston, putting distance between themselves and the Colonel.

For their actions in this rescue, Still and his accomplices were charged with assault. Williamson was charged with abducting slaves. When he further refused to produce the Johnsons in court, a federal judge jailed Williamson for contempt.

Philadelphians were shocked by the judge's action. The case brought the troublesome issue of slavery right into the lives of ordinary citizens. "What has the North to do with slavery?" was a slogan common among Northerners who wanted to ignore the problem. The actions in their own city answered that question.

At the trial of Still and five other blacks, Jane Johnson herself appeared, whisked in and out by white female abolitionists. She testified that she was not "kidnapped" by the action committee. "I

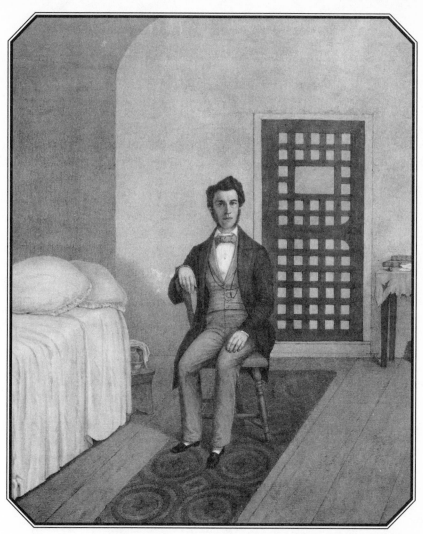

Passmore Williamson in Moyamensing Prison

went away of my own free will. I always wished to be free and meant to be free when I came North," she said. "I had rather die than go back."

Still was acquitted, Williamson was freed after three months, and two black men served a week in jail for assault and battery (putting a hand) on Colonel Wheeler. Throughout the rest of the decade, Northerners could not close their eyes as more fugitives from misery appeared in their midst.

Such was the group of twenty-eight who were wending their way north in the fall of 1857, a group that again tested the strength of black and white cooperation. Three families were part of the escape, including nine children. They left Dorchester County on October 24th in a rainstorm, one father carrying a baby and young child; other children had bare feet.

Another large group had also escaped that month and Dorchester County slaveowners were on the alert. Determining not to be captured, the escaping adults had armed themselves with revolvers, pistols, sword canes, butcher knives, a bowie knife and a "paw," a weapon with iron prongs.

Their food soon gave out, however, and the children became sick. They pushed on for seven days, finally reaching Wilmington. When Garrett first writes of them, a boy has been separated from the group.

"The man who has them in charge informed me there were 27 safe and one boy lost during the night, about 14 years of age, without shoes," he told Still; "we have felt some anxiety about him, for fear he may be taken up and betray the rest....I have several out looking for the lad." (Garrett never mentions whether the boy was found, but there is no sign he betrayed the group.)

On the way they had also been attacked, not by slavecatchers but by several Irishmen with clubs. The Irish were the newest immigrant group in the cities of the North, and they feared competition for jobs from free blacks and escaping slaves. Although he was a pacifist, Garrett related the event with some satisfaction in his letter to Still: "...one of them [the Irish] was shot in the forehead,

the ball entering to the skull bone, and passing under the skin part-
ly around the head. My informant says he is likely to recover, but
it will leave an ugly mark it is thought, as long as he lives. We have
not been able to learn, whether the party [of Irish] was on the look
out for them [the fugitives], or whether they were rowdies out on
a Hallow-eve frolic; but be it which it may, I presume they will be
more cautious hereafter, how they trifle with such."

Garrett passed the group on through Chester County, separating the twenty-eight into smaller parties. As Still received pieces of
information from their various hosts, he decided that the group
should be sent on to Canada: "Far better it will be for them in
Canada, this winter, where they can procure plenty of work than
it would be in Pa., where labor will be scarce and hands plenty,
with the usual amount of dread & danger hanging over the head
of the Fugitive...."

On their way they passed through Still's hands. "They came to
the Vigilance Committee in a very sad plight," he recorded, "—in
tattered garments, hungry, sick, and penniless." He sheltered some
in his home; "they were kindly clothed, fed, doctored, and sent on
their way rejoicing."

"Sent on their way rejoicing." It was a phrase abolitionists used
often to describe the relief of the fugitives when they reached freedom. Many wrote back from Canada to thank William Still.
Knowing of his careful recordkeeping, they also asked for help in
locating relatives left behind. Nat Amby was one of the sixty who
had passed through that November.

"Mr. Still Please Look on your Book and you will find my
name on your Book," he wrote from Auburn, New York. "They
was eleven of us [,] children and all [,] when we came through and

I feal interested about my Brothers I have never heard from since I Left home you will Please Be Kind annough to attend to this Letter…."

John Scott had also come that month: "I left your house Nov. 3rd, 1857, for Canada…" He expected his wife to be passing through the city and wanted Still to send her on to Montreal with specific directions as to how she could find him there.

Still himself visited the black communities in Canada in 1855. Southerners claimed that freed slaves suffered in the North, and Still was sent on a fact-finding mission for the *New York Tribune*. As was the custom of the day, he carried letters of introduction from men such as Samuel Rhoads, Thomas Garrett's cousin. The letters described him as "a worthy and useful man," "a sincere practical advocate of the cause of human rights," a man of "plain good sense," and "thorough integrity."

As these letters attest, Still was gifted in his ability to gain the respect of both races. He was known in the black churches of Philadelphia, on the docks, in the Friends Meeting at Longwood, and in the meetings of the Anti-Slavery Society as a man who could be trusted.

Likewise, Garrett was remarkable at that time for his staunch belief in equality. "I am, as ever thy friend," Garrett closed his letters to Still.

"Esteemed Friend," he confided on August 21, 1858. "This is my 69th birthday, and I do not know any better way to celebrate it in a way to accord with my feelings, then to send to thee two fugitives, man and wife…."

The link the two men forged—between abolitionists and fugitives—overcame briefly the far more ordinary separation of the races.

Danger on the Road

Wilmington, 12th mo. 1st, 1860

RESPECTED *Friend, William Still:*
...There is now much more risk on the road...than there has been for several months past, as we find that some poor, worthless wretches are constantly on the look out on two roads that they [fugitives] cannot well avoid...

Thomas Garrett wrote often about danger on the Road between 1858 and 1860. In the border states of Pennsylvania, Delaware, and Maryland, escaped slaves, abolitionists, slaveholders, and slavecatchers lived too close together for comfort. The "wretches" he mentioned were bounty hunters, people willing to report a fugitive in hopes of receiving a reward. As traffic on the Road increased and as the Underground operated more openly, the risk of betrayal increased, too. Garrett's letters were sometimes anxious but also combative. They recounted rescues barely accomplished and traps narrowly avoided.

In August, 1858, Garrett was worried about a woman whose husband was waiting for her in Wilmington, "as there is great commotion just now in the neighborhood where she resides." The commotion was a betrayal by a black man who had posed as a guide but led eight fugitives to white men waiting to capture them.

The man's wife avoided the commotion and arrived in Wilmington, but the couple encountered another obstacle. A guide, A. Allen, was trying to hustle them onto a train for Philadelphia. "A. Allen had charge of them; he had kept them out of sight at the depot here till the cars should be ready to start, in charge of a friend, while he kept a lookout and got a ticket," Garrett recounted. "When the Delaware cars arrived, who should step out but the masters of both man and woman (as they had belonged to different persons)...."

The masters knew Allen and he knew them, so he left in a different direction from where the couple "were secreted, and got round to them and hurried them off to a place of safety." Allen was afraid to take the couple home with him for fear the masters would have his house searched. By mingling them with a crowd going to Pennsylvania on Sunday, the Wilmington Underground smuggled them out of town.

Another group "caused me such anxiety," Garrett wrote. "They were within twenty miles of here on sixth day last, and by agreement I had a man out all seventh day night watching for them, to pilot them safely, as 1,000 dollars reward was offered for four of the five; and I went several miles yesterday in the country to try to learn what had become of them, but could not hear of them."

The five soon turned up. After Garrett returned from looking for them, a "man of tried integrity" called to say they had arrived at his house about midnight. Garrett then employed the man to pilot them to a place of safety in Pennsylvania.

The risk was not confined to the fugitives. "I have a mixture of good and bad news for you," Garrett wrote in September, 1858. The good news was passing on more fugitives. The bad news concerned an "old scoundrel."

A slaveowner had written to Garrett asking for his aid in getting seven of his own slaves into a free state. It was a curious request, so Garrett was wary, but he agreed to help if the man would bring the slaves to him. Wisely, Garrett refused to send for them himself, and the slaves were not brought.

"The plan," Garrett learned soon enough, was "a trap set to catch one of our colored men and me likewise, but it was no go. I suspected him from the first...."

When the slaveowner was foolish enough to try again, with five more slaves, Garrett wrote him a letter, "letting him know just what I thought of him."

It was no surprise that slaveholders wanted to entrap Thomas Garrett. Hundreds of slaves were fleeing border states like Maryland, hurting the slave-based economies, and his role was well known. Garrett was very careful, however, to stay within the law; he never enticed slaves to escape but only aided them once they had fled. Friends advised him to leave town for awhile, even to go to England for a year, but Garrett just joked that he had not yet been kidnapped by the Marylanders.

Indeed Garrett could not abandon his station as tension increased. Just as he knew how to stay within the law, he was also adept at using it. When two black boys, John and Elsey Bradley, were kidnapped and sold to a slavetrader who took them to Virginia, Garrett and his friends were able to stop their sale and insist on a hearing to prove the boys were free.

He also came to the rescue of Joseph Hamilton, "one of our most efficient aids in forwarding slaves." Hamilton had been charged with receiving stolen money, money given to him by a girl who stole it from her employer. Hamilton was convicted, but Garrett planned to pay his fine and court costs so that he would not be sold into slavery.

As Garrett avoided traps and worked the legal system, Still also expanded his public role in reaction to some alarming legal decisions. One injustice that provoked his response was an 1857 Supreme Court decision in the Dred Scott case. Scott was a slave whose master had taken him from Missouri for a year to territory where slavery was forbidden. Scott claimed that because his master had taken him into free territory, he should be free. However, the Court ruled that the language of the Declaration of Independence did not apply to blacks, that he could not claim freedom because he was not a citizen.

Blacks reacted in anger to the decision. Robert Purvis made his own declaration of independence. Quoting the court, he claimed to owe no allegiance to a government that said a black man "had no rights which the white man was bound to respect."

Still was more moderate in his response, as he tended to be. He called the decision a blessing in disguise, such an injustice that it would bring slavery down: "great evils must be consummated that good might come."

That same year, however, he was enraged at what happened in the courts in his very own city. Henry Tiffney, a free black man, age twenty-five, was arrested on the streets of Philadelphia and accused of theft. Arrests on false charges were a common ploy of slavecatchers trying to recapture fugitives or kidnap free blacks. Soon the theft charge was forgotten. Instead, Tiffney was brought before the federal fugitive slave commissioner and accused of being the escaped servant of a Baltimore man.

During the trial on that charge, several black residents testified that Tiffney was a free man, that he had lived in Philadelphia for at least six years. They said they had known him at least one year before he was supposed to have escaped. Because they were black and not citizens, however, their testimony was disregarded.

In fact, on the second day of the trial, the doors of the courtroom were closed and blacks were excluded from the audience. The U.S. Marshal claimed that threats to rescue Tiffney had been made the day before. William Still had been attending the trial, "anxious to witness the Commissioner's mode of operation and to show my sympathy for the unfortunate man." He was, because of race, among those excluded the second day.

That exclusion infuriated him as did the commissioner's ruling that Tiffney should be "returned." Sitting down in the evening after the ruling was announced, Still wielded an angry pen, sending an account of the trial to the newspaper. "Thus the reader may easily judge," he concluded, "how utterly unfairly the hearing was conducted; what a slim chance there really must have been for the prisoner; and indeed how perfectly easy the most inhuman monsters can be accommodated, even in Philadelphia."

That would not be the last time Still used newspapers to influence public opinion. As a man without the right to vote, he had to depend on the conscience and goodwill of those who could vote to make changes. Such changes came slowly and a few fiery souls—white and black—were unwilling to wait.

The following spring, a bright-eyed, wild-haired white man named John Brown came to Philadelphia, seeking support for a radical plan. Brown wanted to attack an arms depot in the South and provoke a general slave uprising.

Brown invited the leading black abolitionists of Philadelphia to meet with him at the home of Stephen Smith, a wealthy businessman. Only Frederick Douglass, the newspaper editor; Henry Highland Garnet, a minister; and William Still came. No records were kept of the meeting, but Brown asked his supporters for money and men for the raid into slave territory.

Still was afraid such a venture would end in disaster and endanger the Underground operations. He did not want to participate or help. Douglass was skeptical, too. Brown was convinced, however, that such a daring deed would mark the beginning of the end of slavery.

More than a year after Brown's visit, in October, 1859, a mysterious letter arrived at the Anti-Slavery office, addressed to a Captain Watkins. Such a person was not known, so the letter was put aside. Two days later, on the morning of October 17, Still heard the startling news that John Brown had raided Harper's Ferry, Virginia, with a band of eighteen men.

The raid was a failure; Brown was wounded and captured; there was no slave uprising, and only four raiders survived to flee for their lives. But news of the action raced through the country, alarming slaveholders and abolitionists alike. Federal agents searching Brown's hideout found a bundle of letters and documents. Among them was the note: "Wrote William Still Wednesday."

John Brown

Everyone who even knew of the raid beforehand, especially those mentioned in Brown's papers, decided to lay low. Harriet Tubman, "the woman" mentioned in papers by Brown, was whisked out of harm's way to Canada. Still didn't hide, but he did pack up his pages and pages of Underground records, including Garrett's letters, so they could be hidden quickly.

Just as the excitement was dying down, one of the four surviving raiders appeared at Still's home. He was Francis J. Merriem, grandson of a Boston abolitionist, and he was tired, footsore, hungry, and dirty. Still quickly found money to send him straight to Canada. Then Osborne Anderson, for whom the Governor of Virginia was offering a reward, also arrived in rags. After a day of rest, he, too, was passed to Canada with the help of J. Miller McKim and Passmore Williamson. For once, Still chose not to enter these two fugitives' names in his book.

Three men who thought briefly of trying to rescue Brown from his Virginia jail cell also came in and out of Still's home. The men were fully armed and their mere presence a threat to his family's safety, but Still remained "cool of head." Letitia provided constant care and hospitality to Brown's wife, Mary, and her children when they came down to Philadelphia from New York during the trial.

Brown was tried for treason and hanged on December 2, 1859. McKim accompanied Mary Brown to Harper's Ferry to bring back the body. A dangerous radical to Southerners, Brown had become a hero to some Northerners. On the day of his hanging, the black community of Philadelphia closed their businesses and held public prayer meetings. Still went with hundreds of others to National Hall to hear speakers eulogize the raider. Meanwhile, a mob gathered outside the Hall. They were watched by the police, but pieces of brick still flew through the windows.

Feelings continued to run high after the Harper's Ferry raid. Southerners were outraged that Brown had tried to use force to free the slaves. Most Northerners thought Brown was extreme, but his actions forced many people to take sides and defend his mission. There were times when Still himself thought he should take the Underground to Canada.

As 1860 began, the abolitionists' campaign against slavery was moving rapidly toward a climax. The Underground Railroad throughout the country had not only freed thousands of slaves but brought citizens face to face with slavery's fugitives. The risks taken by men like Garrett and Still and women like Tubman and Lewis meant their neighbors could no longer ignore the treatment of humans as property.

Still and Garrett sensed that something more drastic was about to happen. "I fear that slavery may not be abolished herewith without civil war..." Garrett wrote to a correspondent in Scotland.

"You have effectually laid the axe at the root of the tree," Still wrote to Massachusetts Senator Charles Sumner following his speech on "The Barbarism of Slavery."

In the fall of 1860, Abraham Lincoln was elected president. The South threatened to secede, and Harriet Tubman made her last trip south. After packing up his letters and records of fugitives, Still wondered what to do with them. Keeping such incriminating evidence was a risk, yet if war came, families might be separated for years with only Still's records to help reunite them.

Garrett destroyed the letters he had received from Still. "Thine was received yesterday," Garrett acknowledged to Still, but he kept not so much as "the scratch of a pen." He explained his caution in a letter to a woman who was writing Harriet Tubman's biography: "...living as I have in a slave State, and the laws being very severe where any proof could be made of anyone aiding slaves on their way to freedom, I have not felt at liberty to keep any written word of Harriet's or my own labors...." He kept only the tally of fugitives he had helped.

Still, living in a free state, decided to take a chance. With the help of a member of the Vigilance Committee, he found a safe place for his accounts and Garrett's letters. Among the dead and forgotten, in the loft of a building in the black-owned Lebanon Cemetery in Philadelphia, Still reluctantly entrusted the records to the rats and the mice. Little did he know in 1860 whether it would ever be safe to bring them to daylight again.

9

"Slavery Must Die"

$\mathbf{T}$HE war came a little too soon for my business," Thomas Garrett once lightly complained; "I wanted to help off three thousand slaves." Instead, he had aided almost 2,300 when the first shots were fired on Fort Sumter in 1861. From then on, the task of freeing slaves passed from the fugitives themselves and the Underground volunteers to President Lincoln and the Union army.

Garrett did not believe in violence. He was a nonresister, which meant not resisting even if violence was used against him. He didn't even vote. Because he disagreed with government inaction on slavery, he had refused to take part "in such a tyrannical government." The Civil War challenged his beliefs.

"Every sentiment of my nature is oppose[d] to war," he wrote to William Lloyd Garrison in 1863, "but non-resistant as I profess to be, I have not been able to see how the North could have avoided war. Slavery must die; till then, the country can have no peace."

Garrett went so far as to send on to William Still a fugitive who

wanted to enlist in Lincoln's army: "Am I naughty, being a pro-
fessed non-resistant, to advise this poor fellow to serve Father
Abraham?" he asked Still, who was recruiting black soldiers without any misgivings.

At the age of seventy-two, Garrett felt as if he and other abolitionists were emerging from the "thick clouds" that hung over
them in the 1850s. He was optimistic about the war's results. "A
brighter day is near at hand," he wrote to a friend. "Much nearer
than any of us could have hoped for 10 years since."

Besides the fellow Garrett sent on to "Father Abraham," the
flow of fugitives had become a mere trickle. In 1863, Samuel May,
Jr., of New York asked Garrett for a report to the American Anti-
Slavery Society on his work with fugitives.

There had been so few lately that "it is hardly worth stating,"
Garrett replied, but he sent May the numbers that he had first
begun recording in 1825:

1st mo. 1st, 1860, I had registered,	*2,246*
during that year I forwarded	*33*
during 1861 " "	*22*
during 1862 " "	*14*
during 1863, to 11 mo, 24th	*7*
making	*2,322*

Garrett did not wish to appear "egotistical" by sharing this
number: "What I have done was from principle; from a conviction
that it was my duty to aid all of God's poor in their flight from
their cruel Taskmasters, and I have been abundantly blessed in all I
have done."

Instead of fugitives, the war produced refugees. Slaves fled to
the Union army lines when troops advanced into the South.

Uncertain how to deal with the ex-slaves, one northern general declared them "contraband of war," and that's what they were called. Many contraband were put to work for the army. Others looked to Washington, D.C., as a haven. When fighting raged to the south of the Capitol, as many as ten thousand slaves were made free within a few days' journey. The elderly, the young, even those ill with smallpox flooded into the city.

Washington soon asked for help with the contraband. In the spring of 1862, the Freedman's Relief Association was founded. The association's D.C. secretary wrote to abolitionists in Philadelphia asking for money, clothing, medical supplies, and work for the freedmen. Vessels and captains to transport people to Philadelphia were also needed once again.

Philadelphia activists sent two hundred dollars, but, of course, that was not enough. A Freedman's Association was also started in Philadelphia. Then someone was needed to act as an agent, to connect white support with the contraband. Would William Still be able to help?

At the beginning of the war, Still was forty years old, the father of four growing children. Work at the Vigilance Committee had slowed almost to nothing, and he had been asked, most regretfully, to resign. With faith in himself and the virtue of hard work, he had decided to go into business for himself.

Still already had some business experience. At the suggestion of J. Miller McKim, he had dabbled in real estate, buying a lot for $33, which he later sold for $950. During his first years in Philadelphia, Still had worked in a stove store long enough to learn how to repair them. He also knew that used stoves could be bought cheaply in the summertime.

Still saw an opportunity right under his feet. The Anti-Slavery

Contraband fleeing

Society's building on 5th Street was about to become vacant. Its large room on the street level would provide space for a business, and his family could live on the top floor. So, with less than three hundred dollars, he opened a store that bought, repaired, and sold stoves. To go with the stoves and pay the store's rent, he also sold coal on commission.

Determined to succeed in his new business, Still was reluctant to take on more responsibility. When he was asked to become an agent for contraband, he was also reluctant to be paid. "As a colored man, I feel that as far as possible I should aid in promoting the elevation of my race, and without pay or reward to the fullest extent of my abilities," he told the Freedman's Association. "But I am a poor man and shall be obliged to make exertions to make a living." Despite these reservations, Still took on the job at a salary of eight dollars a month. He opened an employment and housing office for freed people in April, 1862.

Still soon had more "business" than he could handle: within a month, 193 persons had offered employment or help; 74 of those jobs had been filled. However, the D.C. group was having trouble finding captains willing to take contraband to Philadelphia. Still knew just the right person to ask: he wrote to his friend in Wilmington. On July 10 Garrett replied with a rundown of the captains who had smuggled fugitives before the war.

The rebels had burned Captain Fountain's vessel at Norfolk the year before, Garrett reported, and Fountain had become a volunteer in Union General McClellan's army. One of the Baileys [Captain B] was a prisoner in Richmond; the other had sold his vessel the previous fall. There was only one other vessel Garrett knew of sailing from Wilmington. He was not sure of the captain's feelings toward contraband but promised to find out. He also promised to look into customers for coal in Washington, D.C.

The partnership must have worked again, for by September, Still was overwhelmed with applicants. Finding the demands taking too much time from his own business, he resigned as agent and turned over the work to another.

As Still made the change from employee to self-employed and as contraband made the change from slave to free, Garrett watched for signs that Congress or the President would free all of the slaves by proclamation. "The signs of the times for the slaves deliverance is brightening," he wrote to his children; if that happened, "…we may have, what we never yet have had, a United States of America."

The war dragged on, however, and Lincoln hesitated to free the slaves in the rebellious states. He thought holding the Union together was more important. Border states like Maryland and Kentucky contained many slaveholders and had not seceded from the Union; he wanted to keep their loyalty. Finally, after a Union victory at Antietam, President Lincoln decided to issue the Emancipation Proclamation on January 1, 1863, declaring the slaves in the rebel states to be free.

The proclamation meant the end of the public campaign against slavery which had been won at a great cost in lives. No man, woman, or child would again need to be hidden or transported away from a pursuing slaveholder.

In its place, however, a struggle for equality began. No matter how long they had been free, blacks still couldn't vote, serve on juries, be elected to office, or just ride on the streetcar. Even the life of William Still, a man with many friends of both races, was affected by barriers less obvious than slavery.

Besides his stove and coal business, the war had given Still more economic opportunity. Through white friends, he received an appointment as post sutler, or supplier, to the Union army camp at Fort William Penn where black troops were stationed. Still was chosen over several other candidates because of his reputation for integrity. He was needed to break up smuggling and the sale of alcohol at the camp and a counterfeit money scam which victimized soldiers.

Despite the trust of his friends and the success of his business, Still was reminded one "bitter cold" day in December, 1863, that he was not yet equal. He had gone to Camp Penn, eight miles out of the city on the North Pennsylvania Railroad. Concluding his business there, he needed to get back to his store by early after-noon. The downtown train would not come for another two-and-a-half hours, so he walked to Germantown for the one o'clock steamcar. Missing that train by five minutes, he decided to take a city streetcar instead.

There was the problem. Transportation in the city and its sub-urbs was provided by nineteen different private streetcar and rail-road companies. Eleven of the companies did not permit blacks to ride on the cars at all. The remaining eight permitted one black person only to ride on the platform with the driver.

Boarding the car with his white employee, Still paid the fare for both men, but the employer was invited by the conductor "to step out on the platform," as he recounted later.

"'Why is this?' I remarked.

"'It is against the rules,' he added.

"'Who objects?' I inquired."

After a longer dialogue, in which Still claimed that he was a taxpayer, he was forced to take a position standing outside on the front platform while his employee rode inside by a warm fire.

Riding on the platform was dangerous; one elderly minister had been killed there on a rainy night the winter before. Moreover, it began to snow, which "made the platform utterly intolerable." Thoroughly chilled with the cold, Still got off to walk the rest of the way back. He recalled bitterly the words of the Dred Scott Decision, that black men had "no rights which the white man was bound to respect."

Still believed in the power of words, however. Immediately he took up his pen to write a protest to the newspapers, a letter which eventually reached the *London Times* in England. "This car inhumanity sticks to me," Still wrote, "…I shall never forget it."

He was not the first black man to be forced off the cars. The editor Frederick Douglass had once been ejected, and the writer William Wells Brown had been outraged by the same treatment when he returned from Europe in the early 1850s: "The omnibuses of Paris, Edinburgh, Glasgow, and Liverpool had stopped to take me up, but what mattered that? My face was not white; my hair was not straight; and therefore, I must be excluded from a seat in a third rate American omnibus."

Even before his own bitter ride, Still had begun a streetcar desegregation campaign. He wrote an article for national newspapers in 1859. In 1861 he was part of a four-man committee that gathered 369 signatures from white business leaders on a petition for open streetcars. To no avail. By the summer of 1863, when friends and relatives wanted to visit the black troops at Camp Penn, they, too, were forced onto the platforms.

Younger blacks with less faith in the white community's response to reason decided to take direct action. They organized some of the first freedom rides, mothers and sisters forcing themselves onto the cars so they could be thrown off.

As the protests grew, Still organized a large interracial "indignation" meeting at Concert Hall in January of 1865. A resolution was adopted "opposed to the exclusion of respectable persons" from cars. Another committee with white leaders petitioned the state of Pennsylvania to act.

In the legislature's debates, Philadelphia was described as the only city, where The Lord's Prayer is repeated, which compels a respectable woman of color to borrow a white baby before she can receive admission into the streetcars. A legislator told of a one-legged black "soldier of the Republic" who was also abused when he tried to board. Four years after Still's cold journey, a bill passed the Pennsylvania House requiring streetcars to carry passengers of color.

Even as Still's fights increased, Garrett's slowed down. Some days he did not even reach his desk at the store. His wife, Rachel, was often in ill health, at one point so frail that "I seldom leave her for even 24 hours." In 1863 his daughter Margaret became the last of his three daughters to die in their thirties.

His own health was uneven. "I have been suffering very much for two weeks with an attack of Billious, and severe cold combined," he complained in a letter to William Lloyd Garrison, "but with the faithful application of steam and the free use of water, without any medicine, I am now improving. I have kept out of doors part of each day, and today am at my desk at the store again."

For some time Garrett had been operating the store in a partnership with his son, Eli. In the mid-1860s he sold his half interest to one of his grandsons and a young man who had been working there for many years. By then Garrett was earning enough interest on his investments to support himself and Rachel for the rest of their lives.

Meanwhile, he kept up his correspondence. He renewed his subscription to the abolitionist newspaper, *The Liberator*, even when the price went up. He told Garrison, the editor, that he would continue subscribing for "as long as I live, or slavery remains to curse our soil."

When he was feeling well enough, Garrett took the cars to

Philadelphia: for business, for meetings of the antislavery groups, and for visits to some of his twenty-six grandchildren. On one of these visits, the two men who had been passing letters and fugitives for at least ten years met face to face.

No one knows for sure when their first meeting occurred. They may have met, as underground leaders often did, at the Germantown home of Samuel Johnson. They may have met in the Anti-Slavery office on North Fifth Street before the war began.

For certain, they met in October, 1865. Garrett had been to a convention and he stopped at Still's store. In a letter dated October 23, Garrett mentioned "the man I was inquiring about at thy store." The man had asked Garrett for a loan or capital for a business, but for once Garrett chose prudence over generosity. After thinking it over, he wrote regretfully to Still, he had decided he was "too old a man to loan money now so near the end of the journey of life."

That same year the war ended. The slaves were free, and the Union was whole, although battered. Garrett and Still found one last common cause. The Fifteenth Amendment, which would give black men the right to vote, was passed by Congress but had to be ratified by two-thirds of the state legislatures. Without it, a man like William Still could not vote for the next president.

Both blacks and whites argued for ratification. The State Equal Rights Convention of the Colored People of Pennsylvania brought sixty thousand black people to the state capitol to ask for the right to vote. The largely white membership of the American Anti-Slavery Society decided to keep publishing *The National Anti-Slavery Standard* a few months longer to support the amendment.

Finally ratification was achieved, and in April, 1870, huge celebrations were held. The citizens of Philadelphia marked the vote with bonfires, banners, and parades with marchers in black hats and coats, white gloves, and blue sashes.

The Still family celebrated at home. Peter Still had died two years before, but six remaining brothers and sisters gathered in New Jersey at the home of William's brother, Dr. James Still. James, too, had become very successful, despite never being able to go to medical school. Besides William and Letitia, the oldest sister, Mahalah Thompson; her husband, Gabriel; a widowed sister, Kitturah Willmore; a brother Samuel; and a sister Mary came. Beginning then, Dr. Still asked that his brothers and sisters reunite once a year to celebrate the long road to freedom they had traveled.

"Although none of us were tipplers, I uncorked a bottle of currant wine that I had made some ten years previous," James recalled. "We talked of father and mother, and their many hard struggles both in and out of slavery, and their strict discipline in the family…"

No doubt they also talked of the future and of the struggles still to come: the right to go into libraries and go to college and the right to have black teachers teach black children. These struggles would be especially important to the next generation of Stills.

Garrett had received an invitation to celebrate the ratification in New York, but he couldn't go. He had injured a knee getting out of a carriage and was confined to his room for four weeks, unable to walk without crutches. His wife, Rachel, had died two years before.

It would have given him great pleasure, he wrote, to meet his old friends who had labored with him so long in the cause of the slave and to join with them in the last meeting of the American Anti-Slavery Society: "I rejoice that I have lived to see this day, when the colored people of this favored land, by law, have equal privileges with the most favored."

The black people of Wilmington, however, intended to include Thomas Garrett in their celebration. According to one newspaper, "It seemed as if the whole colored population of the State was turned loose in Wilmington to celebrate." A procession formed to Garrett's house. There he was roused and placed in an open carriage with a wreath of natural flowers thrown over his shoulders.

"No man in the country has done more for the poor and oppressed, both black and white, than Thomas Garrett," the newspaper account concluded.

Likewise, Garrett reflected, "No labor during a long life has given me so much real happiness as what I have done for the slave."

Telling the Story

THOMAS GARRETT died at the age of eighty-one in January, 1871. A friend who visited him a few days before his death found him in physical pain but with his sense of humor intact: "Oh, I have become a very respectable man now," the stationmaster claimed.

Respectable or not, Garrett had never stopped advocating equality. As soon as the Fifteenth Amendment was adopted, he said the vote for women should be next. One of his last public actions was presiding at a women's suffrage meeting. He also urged equality for "Indians and the Chinese," which was not a common opinion at the time.

Before his death, Garrett had left instructions about his funeral. He wanted it to be an interracial event, and indeed it was. "Such a concourse of all sects and colors we never before saw," wrote Lucretia Mott, a Quaker abolitionist, "thousands—the street lined for 1/2 a mile to the meeting house where he was taken—and nearly as many outside as in."

Besides those in the street, hundreds and hundreds of both races had passed through his house to take one last look and lay their hands on his face, Mott recounted. She spoke at his funeral, as did Aaron Powell, editor of *The National Anti-Slavery Standard*. Black men carried him to his grave, and his old Irish friend Patrick Holland supervised the ceremonies.

Garrett's death came as a passing of the torch: to a new generation, to women, and to free black men like William Still who could finally have a vote as well as a voice in public affairs. In 1871, Still was fifty years old and a wealthy man, living in a handsome four-story townhouse. His two daughters and two sons were in college or college-bound. His business had prospered, expanded, and moved to become a coal- and lumberyard at 1216-1220 Washington Avenue.

Still had customers of both races, including some of the first families of Philadelphia. People had confidence in his moral worth and business talents. He became one of the two or three richest black men in the city and a member of the Board of Trade. Despite his own success, he never abandoned the struggle for a broader equality, which he waged, as usual, with his pen.

Just three months after Garrett's death, the Pennsylvania Anti-Slavery Society met for the last time. As one of its final tasks, the committee called on Still to prepare an account of the work of the Underground Railroad. Finally rescuing the journals and letters from the jaws of rats and mice, Still began poring through them. He lightly crossed through the accounts he wanted to include. He also selected ads for fugitive slaves and newspaper clippings he had kept to supplement the record.

A seven-month coal strike that year made business very dull, so Still worked full time putting the notes together. He had plenty of material, but he also wanted to include sketches of the activists on the Underground, beginning with that "sturdy old laborer" Thomas Garrett. Still collected tributes written at Garrett's death which he thought "so fittingly illustrate his practical devotion to the Slave, and his cheerfulness—in the face of danger and difficulty...."

Although Garrett was important to include and "the writer" would appear occasionally on its pages, the book was to tell the fugitives' stories. Searching through his journals, Still chose "artless stories [and] simple facts" to tell of their courage. An activist turned historian, he wanted to keep the "heroism and desperate struggles" alive, to keep them " 'green' in the memory of this and coming generations for the lessons which may be learned therefrom."

There was also another reason. Still felt he had to prove the intellectual capacity of his race by writing a creditable book: "We very much need works on various topics from the pens of colored men to represent the race intellectually," he wrote. The time had come "for colored men to be writing books and selling them too."

Cranking out copy, Still sent it over nightly to another friend from the Underground, Unitarian leader William H. Furness, who proofread the entire work. Within the year, nearly eight hundred pages were ready to publish. Still invested about $3,000 of his own money and arranged with Porter and Coates to publish the book, but he kept for himself the right to publish and sell it after one year. It was titled *The Underground Railroad*.

Still had a plan for marketing the book through a network of black salesmen and saleswomen all over the country selling copies one by one. First he sent a thousand copies of the book to editors

THE

UNDERGROUND RAIL ROAD.

A RECORD

OF

Facts, Authentic Narratives, Letters, &c.,

Narrating the Hardships Hair-breadth Escapes and Death Struggles

OF THE

Slaves in their efforts for Freedom,

AS RELATED

BY THEMSELVES AND OTHERS, OR WITNESSED BY THE AUTHOR;

TOGETHER WITH

SKETCHES OF SOME OF THE LARGEST STOCKHOLDERS, AND

MOST LIBERAL AIDERS AND ADVISERS,

OF THE ROAD.

BY

WILLIAM STILL,

For many years connected with the Anti-Slavery Office in Philadelphia, and Chairman
of the Acting Vigilant Committee of the Philadelphia Branch of
the Underground Rail Road.

Illustrated with 70 fine Engravings by Bensell, Schell and others, and
Portraits from Photographs from Life.

———

Thou shalt not deliver unto his master the servant that has escaped from his master unto thee.—*Deut.* xxiii. 15.

———

SOLD ONLY BY SUBSCRIPTION.

PHILADELPHIA:
PORTER & COATES,
822, CHESTNUT STREET.
1872.

Title page of William Still's book

of newspapers where it received many favorable reviews. Then he looked for agents who were smart, good talkers, earnest workers, and especially "wide awake."

"Is he wide awake?" Still asked about a prospective agent. "Does he feel the need of education amongst us? Is he alive to the fact that the times demand that we as a race have got to work our way up in the literary, scientific, mechanical, agricultural pursuits, and that we have got to be willing to promote each others' elevation, to encourage business enterprises springing up amongst us the work of our own hands, the creation of our own brains?"

After writing more than seven hundred letters to prospective agents all over the country, Still soon had more than forty at work, including his son-in-law, nephew, and niece. His goal was to sell a hundred thousand copies. Four editions of the book were published and at least thirty-five thousand copies sold in his lifetime.

Still was delighted with the book's success. He had his hands full night and day with orders and confessed delight in managing both coal and books. In 1876 the book was displayed at the Philadelphia Centennial Exposition. He thought it a fitting contribution to the nation's independence celebration.

His success in both endeavors was the result of hard work, discipline, education, and entrepreneurship, values he passed on to his children. His oldest daughter, Caroline, became the second African-American in the city to earn a medical degree and one of Philadelphia's first female physicians. His daughter Frances became one of Philadephia's first kindergarten teachers. His son William became a lawyer and public accountant; Robert joined his father's business and then went into journalism.

Moreover, Still had the advantage of feeling at home in black or white society. A journalist of the day said Still displayed the "ease and polish peculiar to the well-bred Caucasio[a]n." He never laughed boisterously, the journalist noted approvingly, but with "vigorous sentences and thoughtful remarks" was able to discuss literature critically and earnestly. Using his talent, Still often appealed to the conscience of the white majority when he was advocating a black cause.

To the younger generation of African-Americans, however, Still's approach seemed out of date. During the streetcar desegregation campaign he had been accused of being willing to sacrifice the right of all black riders for the sake of a few as rich and well connected as himself. At a large mass meeting he and his friends were denounced as "base enemies of our race"; his coalyard was threatened with a boycott.

Stung by the criticism, Still defended himself and the success of his efforts at a public lecture. With tough words, he urged young blacks to work their way up in business as he had, "through hard labor, strict temperance habits, rigid economy, and an unimpeachable character in business relations…."

In politics, too, Still found himself out of step. Younger blacks gravitated to the Republican party after the war, the party of Lincoln and Reconstruction. When the Fifteenth Amendment passed, black voters were attacked by Democratic mobs, and a rising black Republican leader was murdered. In Philadelphia, however, the Republicans were corrupt and took the black vote for granted. When Still appealed to the mayor to add blacks to the police force, the mayor replied that Republicans could count on the black vote anyhow and didn't need to hand out favors.

So in 1874 Still urged blacks to vote for the reform candidates instead of blindly following the party. His stirring words won converts nationwide, but he was criticized locally. Finally, in 1881, a Democratic mayor appointed the first four blacks to the police force. Still and Robert Purvis organized a celebration of more than two thousand people in Liberty Hall.

Thereafter, Still gradually withdrew from politics and turned to philanthropy. Wherever money or leadership was needed, he was usually serving on the board. He was also good at bringing white money and technical expertise together with black knowledge of local needs and people. Such partnerships produced a Home for Aged and Infirm Colored People, a Home for Colored Children, a YMCA, more than one college, and a black-owned bank. He contributed one thousand dollars to start a new magazine, *The Nation*.

Not only worthy causes but worthy people received his support. Still encouraged the poet Frances Watkins Harper and supported the abolitionist Sojourner Truth in her old age.

Some causes he would not support. Always a very serious man, Still stopped paying dues to the Pythian Baseball Club because he decided such sport was a frivolous amusement.

Nearing the end of the century and at the age of seventy-five, Still wrote to a friend that he "had to submit without murmuring to the inevitable" and give up the coal business. He still corresponded with the abolitionists he had known, enlisting the help of his daughter Frances when he experienced "a slight failure of eyesight." Because of ill health, however, he was not quite as prompt in answering letters, as he explained to Grace Anna Lewis, a surviving friend and correspondent from the Underground days:

Extract of Letter to Author.

"THE UNDERGROUND RAILROAD: I have examined it with a deep and thrilling interest. It is a most important portion of anti-slavery history, which, but for your industry, research, and personal experience and knowledge, might nearly all have been lost to posterity. Its reliableness, moreover, cannot be called in question. It is therefore not fiction founded upon fact, and embellished by a lively imagination, but fact without a particle of fiction, narrated in a simple, ingenious, straightforward manner, and needing no coloring whatever. . . . . . I hope that the sale of your work will be largely extended, not only that the large expense incurred by its preparation and printing may be liberally covered, but for the enlightenment of the rising generations as to the inherent cruelty of the defunct slave system, and to perpetuate such an abhorrence of it as to prevent any further injustice toward the colored population of our land. It is a book for every household."

WILLIAM LLOYD GARRISON.

JUST OUT.

THE NEW AND REVISED EDITION
OF THE
UNDERGROUND RAILROAD.
BY WILLIAM STILL.
WITH A LIFE OF THE AUTHOR.

244 South Twelfth Street,

Philadelphia, Jan 7 1898

Miss Grace Anna Lewis,

Media, Penn

Dear Friend: Your favor of a recent date was duly rec'd & I had intended to have answered almost immediately, & I find that several days have slipped by, & my design not carried into effect; but nevertheless, I am about doing so as you will perceive within a day or two

Permit me to thank you very kindly for your generous letter and gifts of the beautiful chairs, which I must here take occasion to say were seized very heartily by my daughter Frances Ellen (who by the way is writing this letter for me,) and also I will here state, as you suggested, if I did not wish to keep them, I could present them to Mrs Coffin's school, we appreciate them too highly to part with them, They come very opportune and a fitting Memorial of my friend.

While I have been desirous of paying you a visit, as indicated in your letter, there has been some little delay on account of the cold weather, & some deficiency in health, with a degree of slight failure of

William Still's letter to Grace Anna Lewis

January 7, 1898

Dear Friend:

Your favor of a recent date was duly rec'd & I had intended to have answered almost immediately. I find that several days have slipped by, & my design not carried into effect, but nevertheless I am about doing so as you will perceive within a day or two.

Still died in 1902, at the age of eighty-one, which was the same age Garrett had been at his death. Letitia survived him by four years. His obituary in *The New York Times* on July 15 described him as a man of wealth and one of the best-educated members of his race, who was known throughout the country as the "Father of the Underground Railroad."

More personal tributes came from friends like Allen W. Turnage, whose stove business was across the street from Still's coalyard. Turnage had bought all his coal at Still's yard for fourteen years, and they had talked on occasion.

"I went over to his office one evening to order or pay for a ton of coal, and when he had finished his office work he invited me in the back sitting room, and there we conversed until a late hour."

Turnage wrote that Still seemed to have a "higher calling," that he served not only the interest of the individual "but the general welfare of mankind....In the death of Mr. Still...," he wrote, "the colored race in this city have lost their last great man of this day."

Another writer suggested that his work on the Underground entitled him to a monument. "There are costly monuments towering toward the sky to men of the Caucasian race for deeds not so great nor so dangerous as his acts in the under-ground Rail Road...."

Still needed no monument, however. His book survived him. It tells even to this day the story of two men who spanned a century, who wrote to each other as "respected and esteemed friends," and who collaborated as "friends of humanity" in a much greater cause.

Source Notes

All of the quotes in this book are from real letters and notes written by Thomas Garrett, William Still, and others. Garrett's letters have been collected and published by James A. McGowan in *Stationmaster on the Underground Railroad, The Life and Letters of Thomas Garrett* (Moylan, Pa.: The Whimsie Press, 1977). The man who kept many of Garrett's letters, of course, was William Still who first published them in *The Underground Railroad,* in 1871. (Still's book has been reprinted by the Johnson Publishing Company.) These two books are the most important sources for the quotes in this book. Additional sources are listed for each chapter.

In addition to books and letters, however, I would like to acknowledge the help of two people in particular: James McGowan, who has researched the lives of Thomas Garrett and Harriet Tubman extensively and who first suggested a young adult biography of Thomas Garrett to me, and Philip Lapsansky of the Library Company of Philadelphia, whose knowledge of William Still and Philadelphia history matches McGowan's knowledge of Garrett. Also helpful were Randy Nelson and Paula Laine of the South Seattle Community College Library, Frances Cloud Taylor, Ed Skiphorst of Rutgers University Library, David Morris, Bob and Wyn Klenck, and Jean de Mocko's seventh-grade reading class at Tillicum Middle School in Bellevue, Washington. Thanks, too, to the long-listening members of my writing groups: Vivian Bowden, Mary O'Brien, Susan Starbuck, Yukiko Tanaka, Janine Shinkoskey Brodine, Rose Mary Mechem Gordon, and Terri Miller.

Chapter One: Esteemed Friends

The Jackson story is recounted in Still's *Underground Railroad* and McGowan's *Stationmaster.*

Chapter Two: Thomas Garrett of Wilmington

In addition to Thomas Garrett's letters, *Stationmaster* includes accounts of the 1848 trial and the Hawkins family escape and excerpts from memorial addresses about Garrett. Another source of miscellaneous papers is Helen Garrett's notebook at the Historical Society of Delaware in Wilmington, Delaware.

Chapter Three: William Still of Philadelphia

Information on William Still comes from his own accounts in *The Underground Railroad;* from a biographical essay by James P. Boyd which was included in the 1886 edition of *The Underground Railroad;* from an article by Linn Washington, Jr., in *The Philadelphia Inquirer,* "The Chronicle of an American First Family" (October 11, 1987); from a talk given by Phil Lapsansky of The Library Company of Philadelphia, "Aboard William Still's *Underground Railroad*: Celebrating an African-American Classic," Feb. 9, 1993; from the Pennsylvania Abolition Society Papers in the Historical Society of Pennsylvania Collection; and from a folder of information on the Stills in the Gloucester County (NJ) Historical Society Library, including Dr. James Still's *Early Recollections and Life of Dr. James Still, 1812-1885,* Medford, N.J.: Medford Historical Society, 1971.

Peter Still's story was recorded in a book published in 1856 by Kate E.R. Pickard, *The Kidnapped and the Redeemed.* A more current version, based on Pickard's book is *The Man Who Bought Himself* by Peggy Mann and Vivian W. Siegal (Macmillan, 1975). William Still's account of the discovery of his brother was in a letter to J. Miller McKim, October 1, 1850, which has been published in *The Black Abolitionist Papers,* Vol. IV, C. Peter Ripley, ed., University of North Carolina Press, 1991.

Chapter Four: The Conductors

The friends in Scotland were Eliza Wigham and Mary Edmundson, sisters who were Quakers and abolitionists. Garrett's letters to them are included in *Stationmaster.*

Harriet Tubman's life and work is described in many books, including the author's *Harriet Tubman,* Franklin Watts, 1990. An article by Priscilla Thompson, "Harriet Tubman, Thomas Garrett, and the Underground Railroad," *Delaware History* 1986, 22(1): 1-21, was helpful for both books.

Chapter Five: Escape by Sea

All of these accounts come from *Stationmaster* and *The Underground Railroad.*

Chapter Six: A Nest of Abolitionists

In addition to the Still and McGowan books, the following were sources for this chapter: Robert C. Smedley, *History of the Underground in Chester and Neighboring Counties of Pennsylvania,* Lancaster, Pa., 1883; Frances Cloud Taylor, "The Trackless Trail, the Story of the Underground Railroad in Kennett Square, Chester County, Pennsylvania, and the surrounding community," Kennett Square: KNA, 1976.

Chapter Seven: The Philadelphia Connection

Additional sources for this chapter are the Swarthmore Friends Historical Library for Still's letter to Pennypacker; the Garrett Papers at the Historical Society of Delaware; and Benjamin Quarles, *Black Abolitionists,* New York: Oxford University Press, 1969.

The Christiana Riot is described in Thomas Slaughter's *Bloody Dawn: The Christiana Riot and Racial Violence in the Antebellum North,* New York: Oxford University Press, 1991. The Jane Johnson rescue is described in Still's book and in an unpublished article by Phil Lapsansky of The Library Company of Philadelphia.

William Still's letter about the party of twenty-eight is in *The Black Abolitionist Papers.* Copies of letters of recommendation William Still carried to Canada are in the Historical Society of Pennsylvania collection of the American Negro Historical Society Papers.

"DEAR FRIEND"

Chapter Eight: Danger on the Road

Sources are Still, McGowan, Quarles, *The Black Abolitionist Papers*, and Boyd's biographical essay.

Chapter Nine: "Slavery Must Die"

Still's work with contrabands is described in letters in the Pennsylvania Abolition Society Papers at the Historical Society of Pennsylvania. Garrett's letter to his children is in a supplement to McGowan's book.

The streetcar desegregation struggle is described by William Still in "A brief narrative of the struggle for the rights of the colored people of Philadelphia in the city railway cars...," which he read before a large public meeting on April 8, 1867. A copy is in the Historical Society of Pennsylvania collection. Thomas Garrett's letter of October, 1865, to William Still is in the American Negro Historical Society Papers at the HSP.

The Still family's celebration of the Fifteenth Amendment is recounted in Dr. James Still's *Early Recollections*. Newspaper accounts of the Wilmington celebration are in Helen Garrett's scrapbook, HSD.

Chapter Ten: Telling the Story

In addition to McGowan and Helen Garrett's scrapbook, information on Thomas Garrett's death came from Lucretia Mott's letter, at the Swarthmore Friends Historical Library.

Still's later years are described in Larry Gara's article, "William Still and the Underground Railroad," *Pennsylvania History*, vol. 28, no. 1 (1961), pp. 33-44, Philadelphia: Pennsylvania Historical Association, and in Phil Lapsansky's talk, "Aboard William Still's *Underground Railroad*...." Copies of letters Still sent to book agents are in the William Still Letterpress Book at the Historical Society of Pennsylvania. His letter to Grace Anna Lewis is from the Swarthmore Friends Historical Library collection.

114

Index

115

INDEX

Craige, Henry, 37

Declaration of Independence, 82
Delaware, 3-4, 6, 8, 13-14, 16-17, 21, 37,
    43, 58, 79
Delaware River, 23-24
Democratic party, 106-107
Dorchester County, Md., 41, 76
Douglass, Frederick, 84, 96
Dover, Delaware, 10, 38, 45
Dred Scott case, 82, 95
Duterte, Henrietta Bowers, 31

Eastern Shore of Maryland, 16, 25, 41
Edinburgh, Scotland, 96
Elmira, N.Y., 66
Elwyn, Mrs. E. Langdon, 29
Emancipation Proclamation, 94
England, 15, 81, 96

Fifteenth Amendment, 98-101, 106
Fillmore, Millard, 56
Flint, Isaac A., 38
Fort Sumter, 89
Fort William Penn, 94
Fountain, Captain, 50-51, 54-55, 93
    search of his schooner, **53**
Free produce store, 61
Freedman's Relief Association, 91-92
Friedman, Joseph, 24
Friedman, Peter. *See* Still, Peter
    Friedman
Friends, 15-16, 61
    Kennett Monthly Meeting, 60-62
    Longwood Progressive Meeting, **62-**
    63, 78
Fugitive Slave Law of 1850, 7, 21, 34, 70
Fugitives, 11, 13, 15-16, 20-21, 23, 29-
    30, 35, 38, 41, 50, 58, 72, 76, 78, 81,
    87, 89, 98, 102-103
Furness, William H., 103
Fussell, Dr. Bartholomew and Lydia, 61,
    63

Garnet, Henry Highland, 84
Garrett, Eli (son), 19, 97
Garrett, Isaac (brother), 59
Garrett, Margaret (daughter). *See*
    McCollin, Margaret Garrett

Garrett, Mary Sharpless (first wife), 16,
    19
Garrett, Rachel Mendinhall (second
    wife), **18**, 19, 60, 63, 97, 99
Garrett, Samuel (half-brother), 59
Garrett, Thomas, *ii,* 4-7, 10-11, **12**, 13,
    15-17, 19-22, 35-38, 41-46, 49-54,
    56, 58-60, 63, 67-68, 76-82, 87-88,
    93, 97-101, 103, 109
    ancestors, 15
    business, 17, 97
    correspondence with William Still, 5-
        7, 10-11, 22, 35, 37, 41, 45-46, 50,
        52, 54, 58-59, 63, 67-69, 76-82, 86-
        90, 110-111
    death, 101
    efforts to entrap him, 81
    fearlessness, 20
    funeral, 101-102
    home, 17, 19
    lawsuit against him, 20-21
    list of fugitives helped, 21, 67, 88-89
    Longwood Meeting membership, 63
    marriages, 16, 19
    meets William Still, 98
    pacifism, 89-90
    sense of humor, 101
    69th birthday, 78
    stationmaster on Underground Rail-
        road, 4-7, 10-11
    youth, 15-16
Garrison, William Lloyd, **62**, 89, 97
General Vigilance Committee. *See*
    Vigilance Committee
George, Letitia. *See* Still, Letitia George
Germantown, 95, 98
Gorsuch, Edward, 70-71
Green, Lear, 48, **49**

Hamilton, Joseph, 82
Harper, Frances Watkins, 107
Harper's Ferry, Va. (John Brown's raid
    on), 84, 86-87
Harrisburg, Pa., 66, 67
Hawkins, Emeline, 14
Hawkins family, 14, 19-20, 36, 38
Hawkins, Sam, 14-15
Holland, Patrick, 44, 102
Home for Aged and Infirm Colored

People, 107
Home for Colored Children, 107
Hunn, John, 13-15, 19-21, 38

Indian Mills, N.J., 28
Indians, 101
Irish, the, 76

Jackson, Ann Marie, 3-7, 10
Jackson family, **5**, 36
Johnson, Jane, 72-74
   rescue, **73**
Johnson, Oliver, 44
Johnson, Samuel, 98
Johnson, Severn, 37, 55
Jones, John W., 66

Kennett Monthly Meeting of Friends,
   60-61, 63
Kennett Square, 60
Kennett Turnpike, 59
Kensington, 52
Kentucky, 94
Kimberton, 63, 65

Lambdin, Captain, 56
Lancaster County, Pa., 71
Lapsansky, Philip, 111-112, 114-115
League Island, 55
Lebanon Cemetery, 88
Lewis, Grace Anna, 63-65, **64**, 68, 87,
   107, 115
Liberator, The, 97
Lincoln, Abraham, 87, 89-90, 94, 106
London Times, 96
Longwood, 41, 67
Longwood Progressive Meeting of
   Friends, **62**-63, 78

Marcus Hook, Pa., 58
Market Street, Wilmington, **17**
Market Street Bridge, 36, 43-44
Maryland, 4, 14, 16-17, 21, 25-26, 41-
   42, 63, 79, 81, 94
Mason-Dixon Line, 4
May, Samuel, Jr., 90
McClellan, General, 93
McCollin, Margaret Garrett, 97
McGowan, James A., 111

McKim, J. Miller, 28, 30, 34, 50, 86, 91,
   113
Mendenhall, Isaac and Dinah, 59-60
Mendinhalls, the, 59, 61
Merriem, Francis J., 86
Middletown, Del., 15
Mississippi, 3
Missouri, 82
Montreal, 78
Mott, Lucretia, 101-102, 115
Moyamensing Prison, 75

Nation, The, 107
National Anti-Slavery Standard, The, 98,
   102
Nelson, G.S., 67
New Castle, Del., 15, 19
New Jersey, 6, 10, 25-28, 99
New York City, 72, 74
New York State, 10, 66, 86, 90
New York Times, The, 109
Niagara Falls, 67
Nicaragua, 72
Nokey, Eliza, 44
Norfolk, Va., 51, 54-56, 93
Norristown, Pa., 66
North Central Railroad, 66
North Pennsylvania Railroad, 95

Ohio, 24, 53
Ohio River, 34
Old Swedes Church, 54
Otis, Bass, 12
Otwell, Thomas, 45

Pearl, The, 55
Penn, William, 15
Pennington, Peter, 44
Pennock, Samuel, 60
Pennsylvania, 5, 8, 15-16, 20, 29, 61, 72,
   77, 79-81, 96
Pennsylvania Anti-Slavery Society, 19,
   29-30, 34, 37, 47, 53, 65, 69-72, 78,
   102
Pennsylvania Freeman, The, 30
Pennsylvania Society for Promoting the
   Abolition of Slavery, 17
Pennypacker, Elijah, 66, 68
Philadelphia, 5-7, 22-24, 28-29, 31, 41,